# A Field Guide to
# BUTTERFLIES of the
# Greater Yellowstone Ecosystem

# A Field Guide to
# BUTTERFLIES
## of the
## Greater Yellowstone Ecosystem

DIANE M. DEBINSKI and
JAMES A. PRITCHARD

Butterfly illustrations by Lynn Thorensen

**ROBERTS
RINEHART**

Published by Roberts Rinehart Publishers
A Member of the Rowman & Littlefield Publishing Group
4720 Boston Way
Lanham, MD 20706

Distributed by National Book Network

**Library of Congress Cataloging-in-Publication Data**
Debinski, Diane M.
   A field guide to butterflies of the Yellowstone ecosystem / Diane M. Debinski and James Pritchard.
      p. cm.
Includes bibliographical references (p.   ).
   ISBN 1-57098-414-X (pbk. : alk. paper)
   1. Butterflies—Yellowstone National Park.  I. Pritchard, James A., 1954–  II. Title.
   QL551.W8 D43 2002
   595.78'9'0978752—dc21

                                                                    2002008089

♾™ The paper used in this publication meets the minimum requirements of American National Standard for Information Sciences—Permanence of Paper for Printed Library Materials, ANSI/NISO Z39.48–1992.
Manufactured in the United States of America.

To aspiring naturalists everywhere

I hold at last in my hand,
  Exquisite child of the air;
Can I ever understand
  How you grew to be so fair?
          —Alice Freeman Palmer

# Contents

# Acknowledgments

We are deeply indebted to Lynn Thorensen for her patience and her beautiful watercolor paintings of the butterflies. We are also pleased to present the pen and ink illustrations of Jill Seagard. We'd like to thank the folks who know the butterflies of the Greater Yellowstone Ecosystem and have generously shared their knowledge, including Steve Kohler, Dr. Cliff Ferris, Dr. Karolis Bagdonas, Dr. Paul Opler, and an anonymous reviewer. Diane's students over the years have worked hard on shared research projects. Thanks go to Denise Friederick, Julia Auckland, Erika Saveraid, Amanda Hetrick, Ron VanNimwegen, Leslie Ries, Liesl Kelly, Scott Mahady, Bill Norris, Stephanie Shepherd, Danielle Slattery, Michelle Wieland, Sarah Franklin, Mike Freiberg, Bristol McFee, Bryce Nelson, Katie Horst, and Camille King. Dr. Kelly Kindscher and Dr. Mary Harris provided assistance with regard to plant taxonomy and Dr. Mark Jakubauskas designed the map of the Greater Yellowstone Ecosystem. We thank Boyd Evison of the Grand Teton Natural History Association, Dr. John Varley, Chief of Science at Yellowstone National Park, and Dr. Robert Schiller, former Chief of Science at Grand Teton National Park, for their encouragement and support. We thank the Yellowstone Association for their generous support of this guidebook. Our gratitude goes out to Dr. Hank Harlow, Director of the University of Wyoming-National Park Service Research Station at Moran, Wyoming, for his cooperation and support of Diane's biodiversity research. The Montana Department of Fish, Wildlife and Parks and the U.S. Forest Service also assisted the research by providing housing and we particularly appreciate the support and friendship of Kirt Alt (Montana Department of Fish, Wildlife and Parks) over the years. We remain impressed with the dedication and professionalism of the folks in the state and federal agencies who work on behalf of the critters. Thanks to our editor, Frederick Rinehart, for his assistance and support in seeing this guide into print as well as Stephen Driver and the editorial staff at Roberts Rinehart.

This field guide grew out of research that Drs. Diane Debinski, Kelly Kindscher, and Mark Jakubauskas have been conducting in the Greater Yellowstone Ecosystem from 1992–2001. Funding for that research was provided by the U.S. Environmental Protection Agency, National Center for Environmental Research and Quality Assurance (NCERQA), STAR Grant R825155, the University of Wyoming-National Park Service Research Station, the University of Kansas Panorama Grants Program, the Nature Conservancy, the Grand Teton Natural History Association, and the Iowa State University Experiment Station. Although the work described in this guide has been funded in part by the EPA, it has not been subjected to the Agency's peer review and therefore does not necessarily reflect the views of the Agency, and no official endorsement should be inferred. This publication is identified as No. J-19545 of the Iowa Agriculture and Home Economics Experiment Station, Ames, Iowa, Project 3377, and supported by Hatch Act and State of Iowa funds.

# 1

# Why Watch Butterflies?

In the summer of 1871, a scientific expedition under the leadership of Frederick Vandiver Hayden came to Yellowstone to properly map the area of the upper Yellowstone River, and to document the rumored existence of weird and fantastic thermal features. While the mapmakers took their measurements, zoologist Campbell Carrington and expedition member William B. Logan collected butterflies. Carrington, recalled fellow traveler Henry Elliot, "was the most amiable courteous fellow that ever lived and he was a great favorite in the Camp." He helped Elliott to record the depth soundings of Yellowstone Lake, and consequently the expedition named Carrington Island for him. Carrington and Logan carried out many other duties, including standing guard over the horses at night, perhaps protecting them from bears or just ensuring that they did not stray. During the early part of the expedition, Logan brought back to camp a large rattlesnake of interest to Professor George Nelson Allen, a geologist and natural historian from Oberlin College. We know that Carrington hunted fossils for geologist Albert C. Peale, who also accompanied the expedition. Carrington and Logan's attention to butterflies, fossils, and snakes tells us something about science during this time period. Natural history encompassed most things in the study of life, and often involved a thrilling and challenging field investigation of the natural world.[1] Why watch butterflies? Just as our predecessors, we are curious about nature and want to understand and make sense of the miraculous swirl of life about us.

Before the study of living creatures became segregated into entomology, zoology, mammalogy and all the other "-ologies," a person of that time could say with confidence that they studied "natural history." Even until about 1930, a scientist working for a federal agency could claim relative competence in dissecting a big-game specimen (looking for disease) as well as in assessing the condition of a range. From the turn of the century, however, biology became less the study of nature in the field and more oriented toward laboratory techniques. Very recently, conservation biologists have advocated a re-awakening of the natural historian's broad view and integrated understanding of wild creatures. We now use the term "biodiversity" to encompass the diversity of species, habitats, and genes in the natural world, but in many ways the current documentation of species distribution patterns is not unlike the work of the natural historians of the nineteenth century. Today, habitat fragmentation and loss are often the motivating forces as we document what is left of the natural world. When we watch butterflies, we can experience some of the same thrills of discovery and part of the vision that motivated the naturalists of the nineteenth century.

The meanings scientists take from field studies have changed since the heyday of natural history. In 1871, scientists wanted to catalog, name and describe the natural world as it unfolded before the curious members of expeditions to parts "unknown." Today, scientists seek to monitor changing species distributions to assess the effects of human-induced habitat modification or changes in climate. Because butterflies are diverse in species number, relatively easily identified in the field, and often specific in their habitat needs, data from studies of butterflies can be used for a variety of purposes.

Clearly, there are scientific as well as non-scientific reasons to watch and study butterflies. Some of the better reasons to watch butterflies, in fact, are extra-scientific. As we tell our children, it is simply fun to do! Our students and family have often been struck with wonder, for example, at the flight of a butterfly. Butterflies seem to have a reputation as fluttery, wispy, and purposeless flyers. They have been called "the frail children of the air."[2] A more accurate portrayal would describe their strong and directed flight. Even in strong breezes, they are quite capable of going where they like, flying upwind as well as downwind, taking advantage of topography and the wind patterns among trees and other features of the landscape. In short, butterflies are expert aviators.

The aesthetic rewards of witnessing the beauty in life on earth comprise another compelling reason to observe these insects. Butterflies are wonderful creatures that bring color and delight to our lives. In the garden, many people take satisfaction in cultivating an environment where these colorful visitors find refuge and sustenance. In the wild, we are able to witness parts of a natural flow of events much larger than ourselves. Butterflies have long seized human imaginations. The ancient Greeks, for example, referred to the human soul as well as butterflies with the word "psyche." The mythic images associated with butterfly names—especially Satyrs and Nymphs—add a layer of human memory to nature's landscape.

Butterfly watcher Robert Michael Pyle notes that "one cannot become a butterfly lover without at the same time growing sensitive to the animals, plants, soils, landforms, weather, and climate—and the habitats they all make up together."[3] In other words, when we spend time watching the Lepidoptera (butterflies and moths), we become immersed in the landscape and more attuned to the comings and goings of an amazing variety of living things we've never noticed before. Spending a great deal of time observing nature is something the nineteenth century naturalists profited from. When we invest time and energy watching butterflies, we become natural historians of our own time. At the same moment, we become ecologists, noticing some of the same intricate relationships in nature that fascinated Charles Darwin, Alfred Russell Wallace, and other observers of nature. We watch butterflies, in part, to become aware of nature's entangled relationships.

In preparing this guidebook, we've found inspiration and we've added notes of interest from recent guidebooks and from historical sources, including W. J. Holland's *The Butterfly Book* (1905), Clarence Weed's *Butterflies Worth Knowing* (1917), and John H. and Anna B. Comstock's *How to Know the Butterflies* (1904). Naturalists who studied the life histories of butterflies in North America during the late nineteenth century included Theodore Mead, Henry Edwards, William Saunders, and most famously, William Edwards and Samuel Scudder. Edwards and Scudder both published early guides to the butterflies of North America, but other authors including William Holland and Clarence M. Weed successfully popularized interest in butterflies within a larger nature study movement at the turn of the twentieth century.

Clarence Weed was associated with the State Normal School (where teachers were trained) in Lowell, Massachusetts, and his career demonstrates the breadth of natural history study. He was the author of several books including *Nature Biographies: The Lives of Some Everyday Butterflies, Moths, Grasshoppers, and Flies* (first published in 1901), *The Flower Beautiful* (1903), *Birdlife Stories* (1904), *Birds in Their Relations to Man: A Manual of Economic Ornithology* (1912), and *Seeing Nature First* (1913). Weed's popular *Butterflies Worth Knowing* was reprinted no less than seven times from its original publication in 1917 to its last printing in 1928. These guides exemplified the natural history tradition, discussing the life history, distribution, and interesting peculiarities of each species. These books also engaged readers through charming anecdotes from field and forest and through poetry and beautiful illustrations. We are particularly fond of Clarence M. Weed's contribution to the Little Nature Library Series, *Butterflies Worth Knowing.* Opposite the title page of Weed's book, the first illustration features the lovely Regal Fritillary (*Speyeria idalia*), the prairie-dependent species biologists are attempting to re-introduce on the Neal Smith National Wildlife Refuge near Des Moines, Iowa. We hope that anyone using this guide will take delight not only in the details of nature, but also allow the particulars to enhance their larger sense of wonder in nature.

## NOTES

1. Marlene Deahl Merrill, *Yellowstone and the Great West* (Lincoln: University of Nebraska Press, 1999), pp. 74, 150–153, 214–215.
2. Unknown source cited in Clarence M. Weed, *Butterflies Worth Knowing* (New York: Doubleday, Page & Co., 1917, 1925), p. 171.
3. Robert Michael Pyle, *Handbook for Butterfly Watchers* (Boston: Houghton Mifflin, 1992).

# 2

# The Pursuit of Ephemeral Beauty

There's no doubt; it is pure fun to watch butterflies in the field. And the Greater Yellowstone Ecosystem (GYE) is an area of especially high butterfly diversity because of the large range of elevations and the topographic diversity in the landscape. Here we offer a few cautions and simple instructions about observing these excellent flyers.

Please note that collecting or netting butterflies is prohibited in the national parks. Therefore, when you are in Grand Teton or Yellowstone National Parks, you must enjoy the beauty and charms of butterflies by method of observation alone. The U.S. Forest Service has also become more attuned to insect collectors in the past decade, so check in with the local Forest Service office for the required permits before netting or collecting butterflies on Forest Service lands. Refraining from netting or collecting is not a hardship; rather, it is simply an opportunity to observe a good number of the Lepidoptera on their own terms in a spectacular physical location. We agree with Millie Miller and Cyndi Nelson, authors of the wonderful guidebook *Painted Ladies,* to urge folks to "collect on film, not on pins." When Clarence Weed wrote *Butterflies Worth Knowing* in 1917, he advised that to get a photograph, the enthusiast needed to first secure the caterpillar in order to catch the moment as the butterfly emerged from the chrysalis, just before it took wing. Today, taking good photographs is much easier and can be accomplished by amateurs in the field on a regular basis.

In the latter part of the nineteenth century, nature collections were all the rage. Rather than a television, middle class families placed a nature cabinet in their living room. Young boys and girls avidly collected birds' eggs, nests, and butterflies. If you'd like to raise caterpillars of a common species, consult books published in the early part of the century. Times have changed since the days of the nature cabinet, and there are better ways to enjoy the beauties of nature. Lepidopterist Robert Michael Pyle, author of *Handbook for Butterfly Watching*, extols the virtues of simply watching butterflies, an avocation every bit as stimulating and intellectually engaging as catching or collecting. Jeffrey Glassberg, author of a recent field guide entitled *Butterflies through Binoculars*, has opened our eyes to a new standard of non-invasive butterfly observation.

Fishermen and fishery managers have discovered that the immense popularity of sport fishing comes at a cost. It is simply very difficult to maintain healthy populations given heavy human demands and impacts. So it is with most natural resources in the vicinity of the national parks. If everyone who came to admire the butterflies took a butterfly home for their collection, soon enough very few would remain. Butterfly populations, even a species or two, could become extirpated in the parks with enough pressure. Scientists argue that taking a few specimens for scientific collections has not impacted endangered species nearly so much as other human activities such as logging or urban sprawl or pollution of the environment. In the main, they're right, but many small collections would add up to a drain on any individual population of butterflies under pressure from other causes. Mitchell's Satyr (*Neonympha mitchellii*), a resident of fens and bogs under pressure from development and agriculture in New Jersey, was finally extirpated in that state by intense and uncaring collecting pressure. For these reasons, as in fishing, "catch and release" has become a useful method of identifying these creatures for scientists as well as the nature enthusiast. One way to learn more about butterfly catching for identification purposes is to take a class at the Yellowstone Institute or the Teton Science School. You can practice your new skills in gardens and along the byways when you return home.

Butterfly enthusiasts who wish to get a very close look at a butterfly that won't flit away can view the "voucher specimens" previously collected by scientists. These sorts of collections can be viewed by inquiring of the park biologist at Mammoth Hot Springs (Yellowstone's headquarters) or at the administration buildings in Grand Teton National Park. Entomology or Biology departments at universities may also have a collection of butterflies you could view. A few good private collections do exist, and the best way to connect with those people is to join a society concerned with the Lepidoptera (e.g., The Lepidopterists' Society, The North American Butterfly Association, or the Xerces Society—see Appendix 1 for details). Of course your guidebooks are an excellent source of photos, drawings, and descriptions that can remind you of what you have seen and aid in more certain species identification. And should you still be in doubt as to an individual butterfly's identity, allow that bit of mystery to lure you back for yet another sunny afternoon of hiking and observing nature's most beautiful flyers.

Where can you find butterflies? Jeffrey Glassberg, author of *Butterflies through Binoculars,* reminds us it's "location, location, location." We are reluctant to advise exact map coordinates to find butterflies, not because we wish to hide choice locations of Lepidoptera, but because it is the search itself that yields pleasure and insight. Whether or not you see the variety or number of butterflies you came for, as Pyle writes, "a day out-of-doors is never misspent." The ecosystem is large and there are many beautiful places to explore on foot. Knowing the general types of places where you might expect to find butterflies, you can proceed to discover for yourself the trails of the Yellowstone and Grand Teton National Parks and the adjacent National Forest Service lands. There are wonders to be found there on your own, and sometimes you may feel as if it were the first time anyone had discovered these things of beauty. To aid your search, you will want to learn about the habits of butterflies, and gird yourself not so much with fortitude, but rather with patience. A very good way to observe butterflies is to make yourself comfortable in a place such as a meadow or hilltop, and wait for the butterflies to come to you. After you sit still for a bit, most critters will resume their activity, and your attention will be drawn to nature's activities at their own pace and scale.

Indeed, butterflies concentrate in particular places throughout the landscape. One of our favorite surprises in the backcountry is coming upon a wet spot in the trail and flushing up a dozen or more butterflies eagerly "puddling" at this oasis of moisture. Butterflies are interested not only in the water here but also in the minerals and salts left behind in the scats of ungulates or horses and mixed into the mud. Other good observation spots include hilltops, the banks of streams, narrow places in canyons, host plants (the caterpillar's source of food) wherever they occur, animal manure, and rotting fruit. A few species will feed on carrion, but butterfly watchers are advised that bears are fond of the same, so it's best to vacate the area immediately. Many of the best places to look for butterflies are in meadows endowed with a diversity of flowers. No doubt, butterflies and flowers are intimately tied together, in evolutionary time and in very practical ways.

The Lepidoptera are active amongst the meadow's flowers, for a very practical purpose, nectaring to gain energy for their endeavors. In the process of feeding, they serve the plants as pollinators. But this is not the only association butterflies have with plants. Even sites with very few flowers may sometimes harbor interesting species. Many butterflies lay their eggs on grasses, willows, or other shrubs, so any site featuring the host plant needed for the caterpillar's stage of life will be a place to observe butterflies at their work of reproducing the species.

Don't forget, butterflies enjoy flying in the warmth of the sun, but dive for the vegetation when the clouds cover the sun or rain starts to fall. In effect, butterflies are "solar-powered," very sensitive to sunlight and warmth. You will frequently observe butterflies basking in the sun, soaking up rays like the most dedicated sunbathers. In his 1901 book *Nature Biographies*, Clarence Weed wrote of purposely disturbing a Mourning Cloak that would invariably land so that its wings gathered the sun's rays at a right angle, noting "the extreme delicacy of perception toward the warmth of sunshine, which these creatures possess."[1] This habit of butterflies orienting themselves upon landing (both species that spread their wings out and those that keep them folded together), generally with their little abdomens toward the sun, is referred to as heliotropism. Your expedition to find and observe butterflies may therefore go very well in the morning, but when the afternoon clouds pass over the Yellowstone country, you may want to picnic and enjoy the view or log a few miles on the trail.

Your child may ask, "where do the butterflies go when it rains?" or "where do the butterflies sleep at night?" The answer is most often down in the grasses, forbs (flowering plants), and sedges, wings folded up and very difficult to find without exceedingly close scrutiny.

How do you catch and handle butterflies? We present this information for park personnel engaged in scientific research and for those enthusiasts who want to become more professional in their studies of insects. (Again, let us remind you that collecting or netting butterflies is prohibited in the national parks and national forests without a scientific permit.) Humans attempting to net some of the best aviators on the planet can be a very humorous sight. White nets swinging in the sun, able bodied adults suddenly sprinting, then tripping and falling over themselves in a blur, outfoxed and outmaneuvered by a wee flying flash of color, make for excitement and entertainment unsurpassed by anything at the metroplex cinema. One thing you really might be concerned about is spraining an ankle while running on rough ground. Every enthusiast must balance the predicted unusualness of the quarry against the unevenness of the ground (and therefore the risk of twisting an ankle), judging how hard to push this particular chase. We should also note that a proper net, which will maximize the probability of capture, measures eighteen inches in diameter with a grip and pole extending at least three to four feet. Smaller nets may work, but a large net area increases the probability of capture and reduces the chances of injury to the butterfly.

An alternative and better approach is to employ patience. It is much easier to catch a perched butterfly than one on the wing. Be advised that once you sweep the net and miss, your quarry most times will bolt from the area at an exceeding rate. Rather than pursuit, try stalking a butterfly until it comes to rest on a plant or on the ground. Move slowly and deliberately. Wearing drab colors helps minimize your presence in the scene, startling your subjects less. On the other hand, wearing bright colors may attract male butterflies looking for a mate! You might walk slowly through a meadow, or simply wait at a place likely to be visited by butterflies, such as a mud puddle. Moving slowly, you will often be able to approach a butterfly closely, to simply observe, or drop your net from above.

If you have caught a butterfly on the run, there is a trick. While the net is still in motion, you must turn your wrist quickly so as to turn the mouth of the net 90 degrees, closing off the entry and trapping the butterfly in the depths of the net. Many times a quick look at the specimen will do. You may recognize the species immediately. To release the butterfly, simply swish the net "backwards" over itself, and the interior of the net now becomes the outside, liberating your catch. Often, a butterfly will flutter to a nearby resting place where you can watch it for a while.

Figure 2.1.   The casual approach. (Illustration by Jill Seagard)

Whether you've managed to sweep your specimen into the net on the run or gotten the drop on the object of your interest, you may wish to closely inspect your catch to positively identify which species you have caught. This is the delicate part. Nothing beats a demonstration of handling butterflies, so by all means ask an experienced person how to do this. Failing that, allow us to offer a bit of advice on the handling of butterflies.

Your primary object is to avoid injury to the butterfly. A good trick is to grasp the very top of the net, while holding the open end with its hoop down on the ground. The butterfly will flutter up to the top (in an ideal world), allowing you to gather up the netting material, closing the butterfly into the small end of the net. Now gently grasp the thorax or middle-body of the butterfly between thumb and index finger, right through the netting. Do not squeeze. After you lose a few that flutter away, you'll learn how much pressure you can apply safely. Push your hand and arm right back out through the

Figure 2.2.    **Butterflies rise to the occasion. (Illustration by Jill Seagard)**

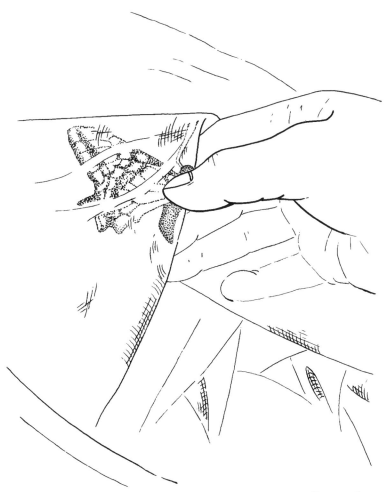

**Figure 2.3.   Grasping gently through the net. (Illustration by Jill Seagard)**

hoop, in effect, turning the net inside out and bringing the butterfly out of the net. Carefully clearing the netting away, you have the butterfly's wings free to the light of day, your grasping hand still in the net.

You will need special flat-bladed tweezers (forceps) to hold the butterfly's wings together without harming them. A type that works well is the sort stamp collectors use (see Appendix

1 for sources of equipment). Make sure your forceps are placed to grasp all four of the front and hind wings together. Usually it's possible to gently close the wings together with the forceps and then firmly grasp all four wings just above the thorax. You really cannot hurt the butterfly with a solid hold of the forceps solely on the wings. If you fail to grasp all four wings in the forceps, the butterfly may flutter about and injure itself. While you are learning, if you do not have a good hold on all four wings, it may be best to release the butterfly right away before such injury occurs. It is important to use

**Figure 2.4.** Pull the net inside out, and grasp with forceps. (Illustration by Jill Seagard)

**Figure 2.5.    From forceps to hand. (Illustration by Jill Seagard)**

the forceps, because grasping the wings with your fingers would strip away the delicate wing scales, perhaps injuring the butterfly.

The wings are covered by millions of colored scales. Some species have textured scales that appear iridescent as the sun strikes them at certain angles. Some scientists think that the scales come off easily to help a butterfly escape a spider's web. It is clear that some specialized scales emit pheromones, or scented hormones that attract other butterflies. Handling butterflies with bare fingers thus runs the risk of reducing the apparent attractiveness of this specimen to the other sex.

So after you have all four wings held in the forceps, now you can release the thorax, pull your hand out of the net, and then use the same hand to grasp the butterfly's thorax directly between thumb and index finger. To better view the details of the wings, you can gently slide the forceps between the left and right pairs of two main wings and gently open the wings to view the dorsal (back) side of the butterfly. Sometimes while in your grasp a butterfly will open its wings. When you are finished with your inspection of the wing markings, offer a finger or a shoulder to the butterfly, which often will sit for a spell with you, or will flutter away to resume its butterfly life in the wild. It is preferable to let a butterfly fly away from you than to simply drop it to the ground. Believe it or not, there are many ant species that would love to bite, sting, and later feast on your catch should they be allowed to do so. Butterflies are often stunned a bit after handling, so let them fly off of your fingers or gently set them down on a flower or leaf. It is preferable to release butterflies where you find them. We would definitely avoid releasing them several miles or more from the original capture site.

## NOTE

1. Clarence M. Weed, *Butterflies Worth Knowing*, p. 35–36.

# 3

# Natural History

This guide does not address skippers or moths. Skippers are butterflies that belong to the family Hesperidae. Skippers are generally small and often brown or orange, with large, robust bodies and shorter wings than the butterflies. You will see many skippers in the field. They will generally appear more "flighty" than butterflies, flying very quickly, low to the ground, and in briefer bursts of flight, in essence "skipping." It's not that we don't like skippers, but the aesthetic appeal of the butterflies is greater, and skippers are much more challenging to identify due to their lack of diversity in coloration. Once you become well versed in the "true" butterflies, the skippers are your next challenge. The skippers are somewhat akin to the sparrows, known to ornithologists as "LBJs" ("little brown jobs"), or to the botanists' "DYCs" ("darned yellow composites"). Then there are the moths. Ah, the moths! So many flying creatures, so little time. The real reason we do not address the moths is that most of them fly at night, and we are so worn out by our daytime adventures that we're asleep before these night visitors make their appearance! You can tell moths apart from butterflies mainly by looking at the antennae—moths have more feathery-appearing antennae, whereas butterflies will have thin antennae ending in small bulbs. Several field guides address the moths and the skippers (see Appendix 1). One of the most amazing things about butterflies is their metamorphosis from caterpillar to butterfly. The raw material of myth and legend, this amazing change in form never ceases to astound the student of nature. During its life cycle, the butterfly goes through four identifiable forms: from egg (ovum) to caterpillar (larva) to chrysalis (pupa) to butterfly.

The life cycle begins (let's ignore the chicken and the egg question for now) with the hatching of the eggs sometime between late spring and early summer. In some species, a caterpillar will emerge in late summer and then go into diapause (a resting stage), overwintering in the leaf litter as a small 1–2 mm sized organism until the following spring when it goes into an eating and growing stage. Other species such as the Mourning Cloak (*Nymphalis antiopa*) overwinter as adult butterflies and thus live for some time in the adult stage. You can examine host plants (the caterpillars' food source, which is highly species-specific for many butterfly species) and find deposited egg masses, often on the underside of leaves. Some species lay eggs in masses or groups, while others lay one egg at a time, scattering them across the landscape. Either approach has its values from an evolutionary perspective. Mother butterflies can be very particular about where they lay eggs, not only on which plant species but also on which part of the plant, high or low.

Emerging from an egg comes a tiny larva whose major mission is to transform vegetation into body mass. During its life as a caterpillar, it outgrows and sheds its skin several times; each stage is called an "instar." Many caterpillars go through four or more instars. During their final instar, a caterpillar spins a silk pad from which it hangs. Now the larva will shed its skin one last time to reveal the chrysalis or pupa. In a few butterflies, the chrysalis is enclosed within a cocoon. If we dissected that pupa, we might expect to find some sort of intermediate form, something between a wormish caterpillar and

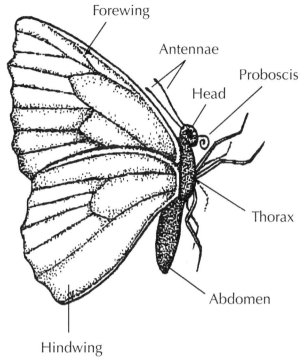

Figure 3.1.   **Butterfly bodies, showing major parts. (Illustration by Jill Seagard)**

the insect with wings that will emerge. The amazing truth is that at one particular point you would find nothing but a perfect mush, with only an inkling of structural forms attached to the inner walls of the chamber of change. This complete transformation of a living creature must rank as one of nature's most amazing phenomena.

By human standards, butterflies on the wing have short lifespans. The life histories of butterflies vary greatly. While there is no typical butterfly, a general average of flying time for many species of butterflies is about two to three weeks. During this short period of time, they have quite a bit of business to attend to. They will find mates, engage in romance in meadows under glorious skies, lay eggs, and fly far and fast. While they do all

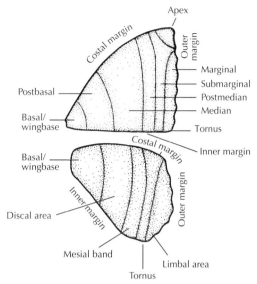

**Figure 3.2. Butterfly wings, with descriptive labels used in text. (Illustration by Jill Seagard)**

this, they will burn calories like Olympic athletes and therefore frequently nectar from flowering plants. Watching the butterflies nectar is good fun—we find it delightful to watch them tuck away and unfurl their tongue-like proboscis, so exactly probing about a tiny flower, searching for nectar. The hidden part of this scene is that all the while, butterflies are acting as important pollinators in nature's grand scheme.

It is hard to be beautiful—living in the great outdoors, butterflies go through their own trials and tribulations, surviving storms and predators' damage to wing surfaces. You may find butterflies that look beaten up and disheveled, which they are. In fact, some lepidopterists use wing wear as a way to age specimens. Most specimens don't have long to live, reminding us of the brevity of all life on earth, including our own. Respect for life on earth, respect for other people and other creatures might be a meaningful lesson at the end of a good day pursuing these creatures of ephemeral beauty.

# 4

# The Greater
# Yellowstone Ecosystem

Yellowstone and Grand Teton National Parks, and the surrounding seven national forests form what has come to be known as the Greater Yellowstone Ecosystem (GYE), roughly defined as the Yellowstone Plateau and elevations above 6,988 ft. in the surrounding region. In the 1930s there was some incipient thinking about animals such as elk that ignored artificial boundary lines, but our modern notions of the Yellowstone ecosystem were indelibly etched during the 1960s by Frank and John Craighead's research on the large-scale movements of elk and bears.

Meadow habitat types at low elevations within the ecosystem, which are some of the preferred butterfly habitat, range along a hydrological gradient from wet willow and sedge meadows to diverse meadows with high numbers of flowering plants and grasses to dry sagebrush meadows. Moving upward in elevation, one reaches high-elevation tundra and rock meadows, extreme habitats with very short growing seasons. A high diversity of butterfly species thrives in both low and high elevation meadows. Edge habitats, such as streams, lake edges, and forest edges are also good places to find butterflies. The key is that there must be some sunlight, and it

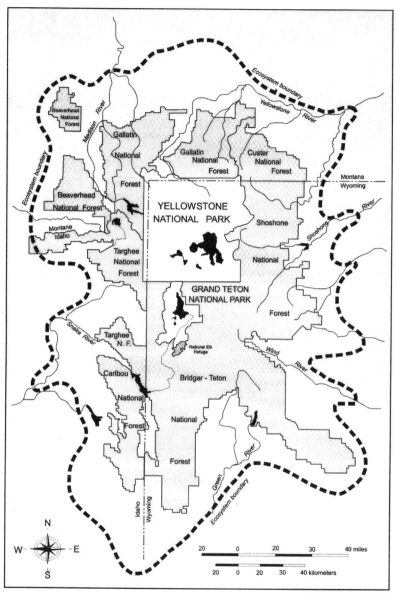

Figure 4.1.    The Greater Yellowstone Ecosystem, comprised of Yellowstone and Grand Teton National Parks, and the surrounding seven national forests. (Map by Mark E. Jakubauskas)

must not be too cold. Forested areas are not generally as good for finding butterflies (and it is difficult to run through the forest with a net!), but walking along trails that have some openings of sunlight can be good places to search for butterflies. Animal scat and mud puddles are often good trailside sites to find these winged creatures as they sip nutrients. In the low elevation sites, vegetation begins to grow during mid to late May, depending on seasonal variations in snowfall depth and spring temperatures. Grasses and forbs progress at a more rapid rate than shrubs in this region, initiating growth and senescence earlier in the season. Vegetation growth is at a maximum in early to mid-July, and by late August to early September most meadow communities senesce. Alpine sites are dependent upon elevation and aspect, starting later and ending earlier in their growing season.

In Appendices 2 and 3, we have included checklists of the species that a visitor might expect to observe within each of the two national parks based upon our observations in the Greater Yellowstone Ecosystem from 1991–2001. Please note that some species on the lists are only occasional visitors to the parks or ecosystem, so don't be disappointed if you do not observe all of the listed species. It is also possible that a few species not on our lists might be observed, because every once in a while a good wind may allow a disperser from elsewhere to be found in the GYE. Just as species' names are continually revised on the basis of current scientific understanding, species' range maps are also continually revised because the butterflies are adjusting their ranges in response to environmental and historical factors. These lists represent the species most likely to be observed in each of the parks. Finally, there are a few species in this book that have not been seen in either park, but may be found within the ecosystem.

# 5

# Species Descriptions

Scientists known as taxonomists organize butterflies (as well as other creatures) into family trees. A butterfly may be very similar and closely related to another species, or like people, be very distantly related and quite different from other butterflies. The careful study of taxonomy reveals a great deal regarding the evolution of butterflies. Taxonomists often base butterfly classification on wing venation. From time to time, a lepidopterist will publish a journal article claiming a certain species properly belongs elsewhere on the taxonomic chart, confusing everybody else, but such is the joy of taxonomy. For serious lepidopterists, guidebooks can be quite out of date in only a few years. The North American Butterfly Association published its most recent checklist of butterfly nomenclature in 2001. Every few years a committee of lepidopterists discusses and sorts out current species descriptions and names. For the casual observer, these disputes are not great enough to cause interference with a good day in the field. Entomologists can be very picky about distinguishing one species from another—there are some species of insects that you cannot tell apart without dissecting sex organs under a microscope. We'd rather pack a picnic basket and head for the alpine zone! This guidebook is as current as possible, using Paul Opler's and Amy Bartlett Wright's 1999 *Field Guide to Western Butterflies;* the 2001 North American Butterfly Association's "Checklist & English Names of North American Butterflies;" Jeffrey Glassberg's 2001 *Butterflies through Binoculars—The West;* and C. D. Bird, G. J. Hilchie, N. G. Kondla, E. M. Pike, and F. A. H. Sperling's *Alberta Butterflies;* and other guides. Part of the joy of watching butterflies lies in puzzling out which species is before you. Attaining this level of detail means that you are becoming a very keen observer of nature.

The insects are composed of many orders, among them the beautiful *Lepidoptera,* divided into *Rhopalocera* (butterflies) and *Heterocera* (moths). Butterflies are divided into six families. Traditionally, they were separated into the "true butterflies," and "skippers" which lepidopterist James A. Scott suggests insulted the skippers! Skippers are now defined as a family with no higher level separation from other butterfly families. Scott gives butterflies the surname "scudders" to describe their flight and to honor the nineteenth century butterfly expert Samuel H. Scudder. Of the six families of butterflies, five occur in the Yellowstone region. Those families are the Papilionidae (Parnassians and Swallowtails), Pieridae (Whites and Sulphurs), Lycaenidae (Blues, Coppers, and Hairstreaks), Nymphalidae (Fritillaries, True Brushfoots, Admirals, Satyrs, and Monarchs), and Hesperidae (Skippers). Skippers generally look more like moths to the uneducated eye and are characterized by smaller bodies, relatively large wings, and straight, clubbed antennae.

The next level of organization below the family is called a "subfamily" or what some of the older guides called a "tribe." An example is the Family Pieridae, that can be subdivided into the subfamily Pierinae or "whites" and the subfamily Coliadinae or "sulphurs." Finally, the classification system gives each species a two part (binomial) name, genus first and species last. This guide organizes the butterflies by family, subfamily, genus, species, and in a few cases, subspecies. A useful source for those ready to move beyond simplicity in taxonomy is James A. Scott's *The Butterflies of North America* (1986).

Here is the list of the butterfly species collected by Campbell Carrington and William Logan on the 1871 Hayden expedition in the vicinity of the Yellowstone plateau, just as they noted in the U.S. Geological Survey report:

*Parnassius smintheus,* Doubleday "Yellowstone"
*Colias alexandra,* Edwards "Yellowstone"
*Argynnis montivaga,* Behr "Yellowstone"
*Erebia rhodia,* Edwards "Yellowstone"
*Erebia haydenii,* Edwards, new species, "Yellowstone"
*Satyrus nephele,* Kirby "Yellowstone"
*Anthocaris ansonoides,* Bois "Hot Springs"
*Colias philodin,* Godart "Hot Springs"
*Grapta satyrus,* Edwards "Hot Springs"

In the list above you'll note the genus name comes first, for example *Erebia.* The species name comes second, e.g., *rhodia.* Third, you'll note the name of the scientist or field naturalist who "discovered" or named the butterfly, or more likely was honored by the naming of a species. Fourth, they noted where they collected their specimens with "Hot Springs" or "Yellowstone." To confirm the presence of any particular species, tradition called for the collection of a specimen that was placed in a museum collection for examination by interested scientists. The first of a species collected and placed in the drawer of a curator was called the "type" specimen. Today a serious lepidopterist (one who studies butterflies and/or moths) might collect a voucher specimen during a biological study to demonstrate the presence of a species at a particular place and to confirm correct identification. Looking through a list of butterflies, you will see famous (and not-so-famous) naturalists listed within the type or species names of butterflies, such as William Henry Edwards or Samuel Hubbard Scudder. A butterfly list thus becomes sort of a who's who of nineteenth century naturalists, especially those with an affection for bugs. Caught up in the thrill of exploring "unknown" places, members of the Hayden expedition certainly hoped to claim the prize of a new species or sub-species, as they appear to have done with *Erebia haydenii.*

Some things have not changed in over a hundred years, including some of the binomial names assigned to butterflies such as the *Colias alexandra.* Other things have changed, including some species designations since the Hayden expedition. *Parnassius smintheus* was for a time known as *P. phoebus,* but then it was revised back to *P. phoebus smintheus.* Argynninae, which used to comprise all the fritillaries, now are classified as Nymphalidae. Modern guides do not list *Argynnis montivaga,* meaning that sometime between 1900 and the present, taxonomists decided it was not a separate species. *Erebia rhodia* has been re-classified as *E. epipsodea rhodia,* while *Colias philodin* now appears as *Colias philodice* (Clouded Sulphur). *Erebia haydenii* has been reclassified as *Coenonympha haydenii. Anthocaris ansonoides* appears in species lists as *Euchloe ausonides.* We're not sure about *Satyrus nephele,* other than the fact that it has simply disappeared from species rosters. The genus *Grapta* is now known as *Polygonia,* included in the angle-wings. We enjoy certain benefits due to all those changes, in that the taxonomic system today is generally much simpler and more comprehensible. In early twentieth-century Europe, for example, two hundred different names existed for what we now call *Parnassius apollo.* Scientists realized this sort of chaos inhibited the exchange of information and delayed the study and understanding of butterfly life. By 1947, Cyril dos Passos and L. Paul Grey had reduced one hundred species of *Speyeria* down to a dozen or so species. Those who thought small differences justified the designation of various species represented the splitters, while dos Passos and Grey embodied the inclinations of the lumpers. If butterfly taxonomy seems complex and ever changing, take heart in knowing that in 1900 it was more so![1]

Below we have listed each of the butterfly species found in the Greater Yellowstone Ecosystem, in taxonomic order according to family. For each species we have noted the wingspan, included a rather detailed description of the dorsal and ventral sides, and delineated differences between males and females (some species show no difference in wing pattern between the sexes while others are extremely dimorphic). The beautiful patterns on the wings are created by the thousands of differently colored scales, all reflecting the light of the sun. In the illustrations, you'll notice butterfly bodies connected to their left-hand wings, depicting the dorsal (upper) wing surfaces. The wings on the right that are not connected to the body portray the coloration and patterns of the ventral (under) side of the wings. If no ventral view is shown, then the two sides are similar. However, in many species, the ventral view is crucial for correct identification. The illustrations parallel the text by demonstrating the dorsal and ventral sides of the butterfly if different, and differences between the sexes where they exist. The butterfly illustrations here are not actual size. See species descriptions for approximate sizes. We also have listed the food sources found in the Greater Yellowstone Ecosystem. Host plants, nectar sources, and other foods are listed if applicable. Adult butterflies are generally much less specific in their food preferences than are the caterpillars. Nectar sources are listed for some adult butterflies that have special preferences. Food is listed in a few cases where adult butterflies are particularly fond of other foods such as sap, dung, or fruit.

Within each of the species descriptions, we have identified distinguishing characteristics to aid in separating those tricky species in genera such as *Speyeria*. We have used the following abbreviations throughout the descriptions: HW=hindwing, FW=forewing, D=dorsal, V=ventral, W=wing, DHW= dorsal hind wing (similar designations for ventral side or forewing), ssp=subspecies, and GYE for Greater Yellowstone Ecosystem. See the glossary for further descriptions of terms used.

As you read through our descriptions, note that many of the species may be identified by viewing them through binoculars or even with the unaided eye. There are some species, however, which require close scrutiny to confirm their identity. This guide employs illustrations, rather than photographs, for several reasons. First, scientific illustrations possess a particular beauty that we'd like to celebrate. It is an art form that goes back to a time long before cameras were invented. From illustrations of human cadavers to drawings of Mendel's peas, scientific illustrators have assisted scientists in illuminating our world. Secondly, a scientific illustration can highlight the particular identifying features that the text discusses. In a photograph, details of interest tend to disappear amongst the numerous features displayed. Thus an illustration is an interpretation that showcases what the artist wants you to see. This interpretive aspect of nature study is important to learn. There can be considerable variation within a species, so as you look at a particular specimen it may not appear just as a photograph in a guide. Your identification is your interpretation of what you see before you.

## SWALLOWTAILS AND PARNASSIANS
## (FAMILY PAPILIONIDAE)

This family of butterflies is characterized by large-sized individuals. The Papilionidae are distributed throughout the world. They have fully developed front legs; tarsal claws are simple (not divided). One anal vein in HW.

### Parnassians (Subfamily Parnassiinae)

In the Yellowstone region, when you see a white butterfly, your immediate guesses will include the Parnassians or the Pierids. In 1905, W. J. Holland wrote that the genus *Parnassius* was included with the Swallowtails (Subfamily Papilioninae) because "the internal vein of the hind wings is always wanting, a characteristic of all papilionine genera." Parnassians are found in dry mountain meadows from the lower elevations of the Yellowstone ecosystem to the alpine zone. Of fifty species worldwide, only three occur in North America, mostly in mountainous environs. Two species occur in the GYE, and they can be separated if you look carefully at their wing scales and antennae.

1. CLODIUS PARNASSIAN (*Parnassius clodius*) (Plate 2; 2–2.5", 50.8–63.5mm) Like other Parnassians, this species has white, semi-transparent wings. The males are distinguished by having extremely hairy abdomens; females have darker, balder abdomens. The females have red in the area of the anal vein. The FWs of both sexes have black, red, or yellow spots. The major characteristic that distinguishes this species from the other *Parnassius* is that its antennae are completely black. Mated females of the *Parnassius* genus can be identified by an abdominal structure called the "sphragis" which resembles a hollow ivory tube. The males secrete this structure after mating to prevent further insemination. The shape of the sphragis is species-specific. Habitat: Meadows, open forest, rock outcrops, alpine fell-fields. Host plants: Stonecrops (*Sedum* spp.).

2. ROCKY MOUNTAIN PHOEBUS PARNASSIAN (*Parnassius phoebus smintheus*) (Plate 2; 1.75–2.5", 44.45–63.5mm) Similar to the Clodius parnassian (*P. clodius*), but distinguished by the fact that wings are covered with white scales and are not transparent and the antennal shaft is ringed with black and white. Habitat: Always in mountains, usually at high elevation and/or in rocky places. Host plants: Stonecrops (*Sedum* spp.), including roseroot (*Sedum integrifolium*).

### Swallowtails (Subfamily Papilioninae)

Of all the butterflies, these are perhaps the most distinctive. They are generally quite large. In a good breeze, they are capable of rapid flight and can be very difficult to catch, but they are likewise noted for their slow and graceful flight. As

Clarence Weed put it, Swallowtails have "the hind wings pro-
longed into curious tail-like projections, suggestive of those
of a swallow." Some people like to compare the long and ele-
gant tails of the Swallowtails to those oversized flashy fins
that automobiles sprouted in the 1950s. Talk about styling!
Weed also noted that the caterpillars of the Swallowtails have
scent organs called *osmateria* just behind their heads. When
disturbed, the caterpillar will thrust this tubular pocket inside out, releasing offensive odors to defend itself. Butterfly
expert John Henry Comstock called them the "polecats of the
insect world." In his book *How to Know the Butterflies* (1904),
Comstock claimed that while fishing in the Adirondacks,
Tiger Swallowtails *(Papilio glaucus)* would flock about him to
enjoy the smoke of his cigar. These species can all be identified simply by careful observation of wing coloration and
patterns.

3. PALE SWALLOWTAIL (*Papilio eurymedon*) (Plate 1;
2.75–3.5", 69.8–88.9mm) The most distinctive feature of this
species is that it is the only white swallowtail in the Yellowstone Ecosystem. Its black bands are thicker than those found
on the Western Tiger Swallowtail (*P. rutulus*) and it has orange
submarginal spots on the HW. The FW is narrow and pointed.
Exhibits ultraviolet reflection. Habitat: Streamsides, open
woodlands, and hilltops. Host plants: Snowbrush (*Ceanothus
velutinus*).

4. OLD WORLD SWALLOWTAIL (*Papilio machaon*) (Plate 1;
2.6–2.75", 67–70 mm) Dorsally black and yellow with yellow
dots near wing margins and yellow patches midwing. Orange eyespot shown by both male and female with off-center
black pupil on hindwing. Upper FW median bands are wide.
Thorax and abdomen with black stripe. Very similar to the
Anise Swallowtail (*P. zelicaon*), but eyespots are off-center
and blue of DHW is more distinctive in the Old World Swallowtail (*P. machaon*). Ninety-five percent occur in the black
form, and some hybridize with the Anise Swallowtail (*P. zelicaon*). Habitat: Semi-arid mountains. Host plants: Sagebrush

(*Artemisia* spp.), cow-parsnip (*Heracleum sphondylium*) and other members of the Carrot Family (Apiaceae).

5. CANADIAN TIGER SWALLOWTAIL (*Papilio canadensis*) (Plate 1; 2.5", 64mm) Tiger-striped Swallowtail. Found mostly in northern Montana, but could be found in the GYE. Bright yellow with narrow black bands and black margins. Similar to the Western Tiger Swallowtail (*P. rutulus*), but the dorsal uppermost submarginal spot on HW is orange in the Canadian Tiger Swallowtail (*P. canadensis*), whereas it is yellow in the Western Tiger Swallowtail (*P. rutulus*). Ventrally submarginal spots tinged with orange. Habitat: deciduous woodland, and parks. Host plants: plums and cherries (*Prunus* spp.), birches (*Betula* spp.), black cottonwood (*Populus balsamifera*), western mountain-ash (*Sorbus scopulina*), willows (*Salix* spp.), and select species of numerous other families in common with the Western Tiger Swallowtail (*P. rutulus*).

6. TWO-TAILED SWALLOWTAIL (*Papilio multicaudata*) (Plate 1; 3.5–4.25", 88.9–108mm) This yellow tiger-striped swallowtail looks very much like the Canadian Tiger Swallowtail (*P. canadensis*) but its most distinguishing characteristic is that it has two tails. It also has narrower black stripes, and the DHW has yellow instead of orange spots within the upper submarginal band. Host plants: Members of the Rose Family including plums and cherries (*Prunus* spp.) and Gairdner's yampah (*Perideridia gairdneri*).

7. WESTERN TIGER SWALLOWTAIL (*Papilio rutulus*) (Plate 1; 2.75–3.88", 69.8–98.5mm) This large yellow butterfly with black tiger striping is common in Yellowstone National Park and in Gallatin County, MT. Dorsally it is yellow with black tiger stripes across wings. The tail is black both dorsally and ventrally. Similar to the Canadian Tiger Swallowtail (*P. canadensis*), but the dorsal uppermost submarginal spot on HW is orange in the Canadian Tiger Swallowtail (*P. canadensis*), whereas it is yellow in the Western Tiger Swallowtail (*P. rutulus*). Habitat: widespread but normally near moisture,

also tundra-edged deciduous wooded areas. Host plants: Willows (*Salix* spp.), cottonwoods and aspens (*Populus* spp.), including the black cottonwood (*Populus balsamifera*), many trees and shrubs of the Rose Family (Rosaceae) including plums and cherries (*Prunus* spp.), alders (*Alnus* spp.).

8. ANISE SWALLOWTAIL (*Papilio zelicaon*) (Plate 1; <2.5″, 69–84mm) Medium-sized butterfly with distinguishing black wedge on costal FW margin. Identifying marks include blue spotting on HW distal edge and orange eyespot with central black pupil on proximal VHW. Host plants: Members of the Carrot Family (Apiaceae) including cow-parsnip (*Heracleum sphondylium*) and angelica (*Angelica arguta*).

## WHITES AND SULPHURS (FAMILY PIERIDAE)

These are familiar butterflies, and they are relatively abundant. Lepidopterist Clarence Weed designated the groups of this subfamily "tribe of the whites," "tribe of the orange-tips," and "tribe of the yellows." Today the taxonomic category of tribe is not used commonly. The NABA Checklist collapses Orange-Tips and Marbles in with the Whites, but we've kept them separate in our text as many historical guides to butterflies have done. Their colors, largely white and yellow, are uncommon in other families. They fly fairly rapidly and low, and are quite active. Many species in this family will emerge continuously over the summer, rather than in a more restricted period (say, two weeks), like many of their distant cousins.

### Whites (Subfamily Pierinae)

The Whites occur throughout North America. Of about 1,000 species worldwide, 55–60 occur in North America and seven species are found in the GYE. The Western White (*P. occidentalis*) and the Checkered White (*P. protodice*) can be rather tricky to separate, requiring close inspection even for the experienced lepidopterist. The rest of the species are not as difficult after some study.

9. WESTERN WHITE (*Pontia occidentalis*) (Plate 2; 1.5–2″, 38–51mm) White with greenish-gray coloration on the VHW. Dorsal spot in lower postmedian area of FW always present. Ventrally similar to the Checkered White (*P. protodice*), but more heavily marked VHW. Submarginal band of DFW is continuous; VFW subtornal spot is less obvious from dorsal side. Habitat: Arctic alpine, hilltops, clearings, lowlands and roadsides. Host plants: Mustard Family (Brassicaceae).

10. CHECKERED WHITE (*Pontia protodice*) (Plate 2; 1.5–2.0″, 38–51mm) Dorsally similar to the Western White (*P. occidentalis*). White with yellow-green coloration on the VHW. Submarginal band of DFW is not continuous; VFW subtornal spot is obvious from dorsal side. Male Checkered Whites (*P. protodice*) show fewer marginal FW marks than male Western Whites (*P. occidentalis*); unlike females, the male Checkered White's (*P. protodice*) hindwings are completely white. Ventrally male has few or no markings. Female is brownish to lavender on the dorsal side. Habitat: Fields, roadsides, vacant lots, cultivated lands, disturbed areas; very generally distributed in lowland areas. Host plants: Mustard Family (Brassicaceae) as well as Rocky mountain bee-plant (*Cleome serrulata*).

11. SPRING WHITE (*Pontia sisymbrii*) (Plate 2; 1.25–1.5″, 32–38mm) White with fewer markings and more delicate and translucent wings than other *Pontia* species. Dorsally creamy white to pale yellow with DFW cell end bar narrow and notched in the middle and black spots present around apex and upper margin of FW. Ventrally veins on HW edged with olive. Habitat: Open coniferous forest, ledges, outcrops, canyons, alpine slopes, and rocky deserts. Host plants: Rockcresses (*Arabis* spp.) and other members of the Mustard Family (Brassicaceae).

12. BECKER'S WHITE (*Pontia beckerii*) (Plate 2; 1.38–1.88", 35–48mm) White butterfly, but the distinguishing characteristic is that it has a large rectangular blackish spot with curved white center at end of DFW cell. Ventrally broad, green vein edging under hind wing. Both sexes have hind wing veins widely edged with dull green, interrupted by white median band. Habitat: Arid brushlands, fields, foothill canyons and lower mountains. Host plants: Alpine bladderpod (*Lesquerella alpina*) and Mustard Family (Brassicaceae).

13. PINE WHITE (*Neophasia menapia*) (Plate 2; 1.25–2", 32–51mm) This primarily white butterfly has black on the tips of the DFW and a black hook descending from the costal DFW. Females show pattern of black veins around HW margin. Both sexes have network of black veins around the HW margin like those found dorsally on female. Habitat: Pine and fir forests. Nectar: Pine whites nectar on the forest floor. Host plants include many species of the pine genera, including ponderosa pine (*Pinus ponderosa*), lodgepole pine (*Pinus contorta*), Douglas fir (*Pseudotsuga menziesii*), Western hemlock (*Tsuga heterophylla*), and Engelmann spruce (*Picea engelmannii*). Can be a pest species. The larvae of this species are well known for defoliating conifers.

14. MARGINED MUSTARD WHITE (*Pieris napi marginalis*) (Plate 3; 1.5–1.70", 36–42mm) Of all the Pierids in the Yellowstone ecosystem, this one is most unremarkable in coloration. Males are white and females can range from immaculate white to pale yellow or even have the appearance of dusting with black. The wing veins are prominent in both sexes. Female FW may exhibit two dark spots in submarginal area of FW, where male has one. Habitat: Shady deciduous or coniferous forests, forest clearings or edges, tundra, roadsides, other cool and moist places. Host plants: Mustard Family (Brassicaceae).

15. CABBAGE WHITE (*Pieris rapae*) (Plate 3; 1.65–2", 42–51mm) This common garden pest has a broad range cov-

ering most of the continental U.S. The groundcolor is white in males and more yellowish in females. Males exhibit one black spot in the outer median range of FW; females have two spots. One black spot in costal area of DHW is found on both sexes. Habitat: Open or lightly wooded areas including roadsides and agricultural lands. Host plants: Mustard Family (Brassicaceae). Introduced to North America about 1860 (Quebec) and in 1868 (New York City), within thirty years the Cabbage White (*P. rapae*) became a noted pest all over the United States and Canada. By 1917, it was clear that this invader had crowded and seriously impacted native populations of Pierids.

## Marbles

Marbles are named for the pattern exhibited on their ventral side, especially on the hindwing. The Olympia Marble (*E. olympia*) can be separated from the Large and Desert Pearly Marble (*E. ausonides* and *E. hyantis lotta*), but the latter two species are very difficult to separate, even if they are being held carefully in the hand. Some of these species will stay in their chrysalis through several bad years until favorable conditions return. In any locality, marblewings fly for only a brief period in the springtime. Enjoy these harbingers of warmer weather while they are on the wing!

16. OLYMPIA MARBLE (*Euchloe olympia*) (Plate 3; 1.29–1.6", 33–42mm) Small white butterfly with marbled ventral HW and white antennae. The feature that distinguishes this species from the other two *Euchloe* is that its marbling is much less dense; less than one-half of the wing is dark with marbling. Dorsally no distal FW markings as in the Large Marble (*E. ausonides*) except (proximal) discal spot, gray/black dash near FW apex almost halfway down outer margin of FW. Ventrally fewer greenish large veins and three irregular bands with more white on HW than the Large Marble (*E. ausonides*), and a rosy ground tint under HW. Antennae are pure white.

Habitat: Open woodland meadows, riverbanks, open hills. Host plants: Rockcresses (*Arabis* spp.) and western tansymustard (*Descurainia pinnata*).

17. LARGE MARBLE (*Euchloe ausonides*) (Plate 3; 1.5–2", 38.1–50.8mm) Most common of *Euchloe* species. Dorsally ground color often tinged with yellow, at least on HW. Ventrally HW more yellowish green than the green of the Desert Pearly Marble (*E. hyantis lotta*), mottled, looks like mold or moss. To distinguish from the Desert Pearly Marble (*E. hyantis lotta*), use a hand lens to check DFW cell bar for white scales. The Large Marble (*E. ausonides*) has many white scales, whereas the Desert Pearly Marble (*E. hyantis lotta*) has few or none in this cell bar. VHW does NOT have pearly iridescence. Usually flies later in the season than the Desert Pearly Marble (*E. hyantis lotta*). Habitat: Open forest, fields, and meadows. Host plants: Common tansy (*Tanacetum vulgare*) and several species from the Mustard Family (Brassicacae) including rockcresses (*Arabia* spp.), marsh yellowcress (*Rorippa palustris*), and common tansymustard (*Descurainia sophia*).

18. DESERT PEARLY MARBLE (*Euchloe hyantis lotta*) (Plate 3; 1.3–1.6", 34–41mm) Smaller and greener than the Large Marble (*E. ausonides*); markings more clean cut. To distinguish the Desert Pearly Marble (*E. hyantis lotta*) from the Large Marble (*E. ausonides*), use a hand lens to check DFW cell bar for white scales. The Large Marble (*E. ausonides*) has many white scales, whereas the Desert Pearly Marble (*E. hyantis lotta*) has few or none in this cell bar. Dorsally FW discal spot larger and wider than the Large Marble (*E. ausonides*). HW with distinct median vein. Ventrally FW has distal dark markings in addition to hollow discal spot; HW more heavily marbled green than the Large Marble (*E. ausonides*), VHW has pearly iridescence. Habitat: Rocky canyons, ridges, and cutbacks. Host plants: From the Mustard Family (Brassicaceae) including rockcresses (*Arabis* spp.) and common tansymustard (*Descurainia sophia*).

## Orangetips

Clarence Weed wrote: "When one sees a gossamer-winged butterfly flitting from flower to flower on a bright June day it seems one of the most ethereal of earth's visions. One could readily fancy that the whole sight—flowers, butterflies, and all—might easily vanish into thin air." Despite their apparent fragility, Weed pointed out, butterflies endured for millions of years by adapting to changing circumstances. One adaptation of some Orangetips was matching their life cycle to that of cruciferous host plants. The other adaptation was the remarkable marking of the wings. Characteristically, the upper sides of the front wings have a bright orange marking near the apex, but the undersides are pale white or yellowish green, spotted with darker colors and so peculiar that it was called "flower picturing" in Weed's day. A pursuing bird would notice the orange wing tips while the butterfly took to wing, but lose sight of it when it alighted in foliage.

19. STELLA SARA ORANGETIP (*Anthocharis sara stella*) (Plate 3; 1.35–1.60", 34–41mm) Since this is the only orangetip in the GYE, this species can be easily identified in the air. Small butterfly with bright orange apical spot, white ground color in male; female ground color yellow. Apical spot is more reddish in male. Ventrally, there is grass green marbling on HW. Habitat: Aspen woods and meadows. Host plants: Mustard Family (Brassicaceae).

## Sulphurs (Subfamily Coliadinae)

Many common and conspicuous butterflies belong to Weed's "Tribe of the Yellows." Some of these species have red antennae, so in Clarence Weed's day some called it the "Tribe of the Red-horns." The group is distinguished, apart from its various hues of yellow, by the gradual enlargement of the antennae joints, and by the stout palpi. The Sulphurs can be somewhat challenging to differentiate, but with careful attention to the coloration patterns on the dorsal side and especially the spot patterns on the ventral hindwing, one can usually separate them. Males often have broad black wing margins, while females have "windowed" black margins. Females of some of the species show considerable overlap and come in both white and yellow forms, so these are the most difficult to distinguish. Finally, there is hybridization between some of the Sulphurs, so it is no wonder that we find them challenging!

20. PELIDNE SULPHUR (*Colias pelidne*) (Plate 4; 1.3–1.7", 34–44mm) Female is usually white, but may be yellow. Wing border is dark, often incomplete, and broken. Males are pale yellow with narrow to medium dark border. Dorsally wing bases are dark scaled with green suffusion in both sexes. FW discal spot is small. HW discal spot faint. Ventrally heavily dark scaled in both sexes. DHW spot is yellow on male; is slightly orange female. VHW discal spot is red-ringed or all red, rarely with a satellite spot. Wing edges pink. Differs from the Pink-edged Sulphur (*C. interior*) in having yellow (rather than orange) DHW central spot and having darker VHW and base of VFW. Habitat: Tundra, fell fields, subalpine meadows and forest clearings. Host plants: Huckleberry (*Vaccinium cespitosum*) and alpine false-wintergreen (*Gaultheria humifusa*).

21. MEAD'S SULPHUR (*Colias meadii*) (Plate 4; 1.5–2", 38–50mm) This high alpine species usually found above 9,000 ft. is an Ice-Age relict. If observed, you will not have difficulty differentiating it from other Sulphurs. Males are deep orange with a wide, black border dorsally. Females are lighter orange with a broken black border, enclosing spots of ground color. Male has an orange sex mark on HW costa near base. The ventral side is greenish-yellow in both sexes. The HW discal spot is dull white, and ringed with red. Habitat: High mountain areas at or near timberline. Host plants: Alpine milk-vetch (*Astragalus alpinus*), reflexed locoweed (*Oxytropis deflexa*), whip-root clover (*Trifolium dasyphyllum*), dwarf clover (*T. nanum*), Parry's clover (*T. parryi*), and wild vetch (*Vicia americana*).

22. GIANT SULPHUR (*Colias gigantea*) (Plate 4; 1.7–2.2", 44–56mm) Despite its name, this species is not much larger than other *Colias* species. However, it may best be distinguished by the habitat where it is found. It is brightly colored with a distinct DFW cell spot. The male is lemon yellow with very dark scaling at base and a dark narrow border with yellow veins. Females yellow or white; border reduced or absent. Ventrally yellow in both sexes with very little dark overscaling. FW cell spot present. VHW discal spot large, silvered with single brown/red ring; satellite spot is usually present. VFW lacks submarginal suffusion. No submarginal VHW spots. Pink wing fringes. Habitat: Very specific to wet willow bogs. Host plants: Willows (*Salix* spp.).

23. CLOUDED SULPHUR (*Colias philodice*) (Plate 4; 1.5–2.175", 38.1–55.25mm) One of the most common species of *Colias* in the Greater Yellowstone Ecosystem. Its markings are like those of the Orange Sulphur (*C. eurytheme*), but the cell spot is usually smaller. The male is bright lemon yellow; the female can be white or yellow. The female's black DFW border is narrower than male's with smaller light spots and less black than the Orange Sulphur (*C. eurytheme*). Female wing edges are windowed/scalloped on dorsal side. HW discal spot orange. VHW and VFW have submarginal dots; VHW is brownish and discal spot usually has a satellite. Habitat: Meadows, fields, cultivated land, roadsides, and brushland. Host plants: Various members of the Pea Family (Fabaceae) including clovers (*Trifolium* spp.), milk-vetches (*Astragalus* spp.), as well as select species of other pea genera. Like the Orange Sulphur (*C. eurytheme*), the Clouded Sulphur (*C. philodice*) feeds in alfalfa fields. Very common among the Sulphurs, but did not gain a reputation for damage to agriculture, as did the Cabbage White (*P. rapae*). Weed thought the Clouded Sulphur exemplified the balance of nature, in that its ability to reproduce and survive was in relative balance with losses to its enemies and other sources of mortality.

24. CHRISTINA'S SULPHUR (*Colias christina*) (Plate 4; 1.375–2", 34.9–51mm) Dorsally male is two-toned orange with yellow at wing bases and costa, and black shading around margins; also orange discal spot on DHW. Female is usually yellow and has one black spot in the median of the FW. Compared to male, marginal shading is more mottled and confined to the FW only and VHW discal spot is smaller and lighter. Ventrally, it is olive-green orange with a small, hollow black spot on FW and a white silvery discal spot with broad ring on HW. Flies in early May. Habitat: Open areas including meadows, fields, brushland, roadsides, and clearings; also forest edges and sagebrush. Host plants: Locoweeds (*Oxytropis* spp.), and northern sweet-vetch (*Hedysarum boreale*).

25. QUEEN ALEXANDRA'S SULPHUR (*Colias alexandra*) (Plate 16; 1.5–2", 38.1–51mm) Similar to Christina's Sulphur (*C. christina*), but lacks the orange coloration. VHW has grayish-green suffusion and discal spot is silvery. DHW has yellow suffusion on edges with yellow discal spot. This is a prairie species with one flight in May and another later in the summer. Habitat: Open areas including meadows, fields, brushland, roadsides, and clearings, also forest edges and sagebrush. Host plants: Locoweeds (*Oxytropis* spp.), northern sweet-vetch (*Hedysarum boreale*), and red clover (*Trifolium pratense*).

26. PINK-EDGED SULPHUR (*Colias interior*) (Plate 4; 1.5–1.875", 38.1–47.6mm) Male bright yellow; wing bases not dark scaled. Black border on FW at apex, narrower on outer margin: Narrow dark border on HW. Female usually yellow (but can be white) and dorsally has narrower dark border without scalloped wing margins. Ventrally brightly colored with minimal dark scaling in both sexes. VHW discal spot white with red ring, rarely with satellite spot. DFW cell spot small, sometimes nearly absent. DHW spot present. This species has conspicuous bright pink wing edges (but note that despite its common name, the Pink-edged Sulphur (*C. interior*) is NOT the only species to exhibit this trait). Habitat: Brush-

lands; often in burned-over areas where huckleberry grows. Host plants: Huckleberry (*Vaccinium cespitosum*). The famous naturalist Louis Agassiz introduced the Pink-edged Sulphur to the world of science when he described it while on a field expedition to the northern edge of Lake Superior. This species lives within a narrow band around fifty degrees northern latitude, extending from the eastern states almost to the Pacific Ocean. Its range is primarily north of the GYE, but it may be found here.

27. ORANGE SULPHUR (*Colias eurytheme*) (Plate 4; 1.375–2.25", 34.9–57.15mm) Males of this species are distinguished by their bright egg-yolk orange color. Females can be orange or white and have an irregular cell border. Similar to the Clouded Sulphur (*C. philodice*) in markings. Wide black border, with yellow veins. DFW cell spot extremely black and present in both sexes. Ventral submarginal spots prominent in both sexes. HW discal spot silver, with two concentric dark rings and a small satellite spot above. This species is migratory and does not overwinter in the Greater Yellowstone Ecosystem. Habitat: Fields, meadows, cultivated lands, roadsides. Host plants: Many native plants in the Pea Family (Fabaceae). Many species of locoweeds (*Oxytropis* spp.) or milk-vetches (*Astragalus* spp.), lupines (*Lupinus* spp.), alfalfa (*Medicago sativa*), clovers (*Trifolium* spp.), and vetches (*Vicia* spp.); select species of other genera as well. Weed called the Orange Sulphur "essentially a tropical species." Now you know why it does not spend the winter in Wyoming.

## GOSSAMER-WING BUTTERFLIES; ALSO CALLED BLUES, COPPERS, AND HAIRSTREAKS (FAMILY LYCAENIDAE)

Many Yellowstone species belong to this subfamily. The Lycaenids encompass a large number of species and are distributed throughout the world. In 1917, Clarence Weed described them as "winged sprites, playing everywhere." He extolled the Gossamer-wings as the "daintiest and most delicate of all our butterflies . . . their wings thin and of exquisite beauty." Those who try to handle these species will soon understand how delicate they are. They are small butterflies with notched eyes at the base of their antennae. Sexes are often very different on the dorsal side, but alike on the ventral side. They have small bodies, and when you look at them directly head-on, you'll note the face is narrower than its height. Many Lycaenid species have very slender projections trailing off the hind wings. Upon alighting, adults of many species have the habit of rubbing their hind wings together; some say this may be a defense, drawing attention away from the head. Clarence Weed thought it simply a sign of liveliness. Many Lycaenids are ant-loving (myrmecophilous). These caterpillars create a special substance that attracts ants. It is thought that the ants then protect the caterpillars against other predators.

### Blues (Subfamily Polyommatinae)

Most of these species are indeed beautiful shades of blue, and they are on the small side. Spines on tarsi undersides appear in rows rather than clusters as do the Coppers, and the spines are fewer in number. Their bodies are generally slender, and the undersides of the wings are dotted in a fashion characteristic of the species.

28. DOTTED BLUE (*Euphilotes enoptes ancilla*) (Plate 5; .625–1", 16–25mm) Dorsally males are deep blue; females are copper brown. Male's black upper FW border is wider than female's. Ventrally it is blue-gray to dark-gray with prominent black dots (hence the name) in straight rows. The HW margin has a line of orange dorsally on the female and ventrally on both sexes. Habitat: Open woodland and sagebrush. Food: Adults sip flower nectar and mud. Host plants: Sulphur buckwheat (*Eriogonum umbellatum*).

29. SPRING AZURE (*Celastrina ladon*) (Plate 5; .875–1.25", 22.2–31.75mm) Dorsally deep blue or violet blue, with a thick black border of FW. Ventrally silvery white with faint gray and black checkered border. Gray and dark gray variable spotting. Habitat: forest, brushland, groves, and parks. Food: Flower nectar, mud, dung, etc. Host plants: Trees and shrubs of the Rose Family (Rosaceae), the Heath Family (Ericaceae), the Pea Family (Fabaceae), and the Aster Family (Asteraceae). This species is more likely to be found in the northern GYE.

30. WESTERN TAILED-BLUE (*Everes amyntula*) (Plate 5; .875–1.175", 22-30mm) Small blue butterfly with the smallest hint of a tail and a narrow dark margin dorsally. Ventrally chalk white with navy-grayish markings; faint orange spot above small HW tail. Habitat: Moist meadows, canyons, roadsides, sandy clearings, and forest margins. Food: Adults sip nectar and mud. Host plant: Pea Family (Fabaceae) including locoweeds (*Oxytropis* spp.) and wild vetch (*Vicia americana*).

31. SHASTA BLUE (*Plebejus shasta*) (Plate 8; .75–1", 19–26mm) Small, dark iridescent blue with dull orange spots on DHW. Ventral pattern is distinctively mottled in appearance and spots are more gray than black, as compared to the Acmon Blue (*P. acmon*) or Lupine Blue (*P. lupini*). VHW has submarginal band of metallic spots. Habitat: Alpine and subalpine rocky slopes, sagebrush flats. Host plants: Pea Family (Fabaceae) including milk-vetches (*Astragalus* spp.), locoweeds (*Oxytropis* spp.), lupines (*Lupinus* spp.), and clovers (*Trifolium* spp.).

32. NORTHERN BLUE (*Lycaeides idas*) (Plate 8; .92–1.13", 21–29mm) Dorsally blue in male, brown in female with black edge. Cup-like orange spots along VHW in both sexes, and partially up VFW. Habitat: Cool zones in western mountains, open areas, heaths, and bogs in northern coniferous and mixed forests. Host plants: Pea Family (Fabaceae) including milk-vetches (*Astragalus* spp.), and lodgepole lupine (*Lupinus parviflorus*).

33. LUPINE BLUE (*Plebejus lupini*) (Plate 8; <1", 25.4mm) Dorsally the male is a bright lilac blue, whereas the female is brown. The distinctive feature of this blue is that the HW orange submarginal band is visible on both dorsal and ventral sides, but there are no markings on the DFW. Ventrally the butterfly is light-colored with black dots and the outermost row of dots has metallic caps. Habitat: Virtually anywhere in the West. Food: Herbs and shrubs of buckwheats (*Eriogonum* spp.) and lupines (*Lupinus* spp.). Host plants: Herbs and shrubs of the Buckwheat Family (Polygonaceae) including mountain knotweeds (*Polygonum* spp.) and buckwheats (*Eriogonum* spp.), Pea Family (Fabaceae), including milk-vetches (*Astragalus* spp.) and lupines (*Lupinus* spp.).

34. MELISSA BLUE (*Lycaeides melissa*) (Plate 8; .875–1.25", 22–32mm) Dorsally blue in male, brown in female. In comparing this species to the Lupine Blue (*Plebejus lupini*) and the Northern Blue (*L. idas*), the major difference is that the cup-like orange spots in the Melissa Blue (*L. melissa*) are found along VHW in both sexes and continue up VFW. These spots are also much more brilliantly orange than Shasta blue (*P. shasta*). Habitat: Prairies, dry meadows, alfalfa fields and waste areas. Host plants: Pea Family (Fabaceae) including alfalfa (*Medicago sativa*), common sweet clover (*Melilotus officinalis*), and lupines (*Lupinas* spp.).

35. GREENISH BLUE (*Plebejus saepiolus*) (Plate 8; <1", 25.4mm) This is one of the more common blues to be found in the ecosystem, especially in wetter sites. However, green is really not the best descriptor of its color. Male is blue dorsally with dark margins, while female is brown to orange-brown. Ventrally both sexes are light brown-gray and sometimes one can observe one very small, yet distinctive orange spot on VHW corner. However, even if the orange spot is not obvious, one can distinguish a fine row of dots and chevrons along the VHW margin that is not present in the Boisduval's Blue (*P. icarioides*). Habitat: Wet areas, bogs, meadows, grassy slopes, and roadside ditches. Nectar: Clovers

(*Trifolium* spp.), bistorts (*Polygonum* spp.), and Asters (Asteraceae). Notes: Great variety in coloring. Host plants: Clovers (*Trifolium* spp.).

36. BOISDUVAL'S BLUE (*Plebejus icarioides*) (Plate 8; <1", 25.4mm) Another very common blue, seen most frequently in drier sagebrush meadows. Male is blue dorsally with dark margins, whereas female can be blue to brown. Ventrally this species is variable, with pale coloring and the VFW has more prominent black spots bordered by white rings. The VHW has less of a pattern of dots and chevrons along the margin as compared to the Greenish Blue (*P. saepiolus*). In some cases one can distinguish it from the Greenish Blue (*P. saepiolus*) by looking for a tiny orange spot on the VHW. Only the Greenish Blue (*P. saepiolus*) has the orange spot. Habitat: Mountains, valleys, meadows, streams, sagelands, and roadsides. Food: Mud and flower nectar. Host plants: Shrubby legumes (Family Fabaceae). Interestingly, the eggs are deposited on the hairiest plants and ants tend the larvae.

37. ARCTIC BLUE (*Agriades glandon*) (Plate 8; .88–1.1", 22–28mm) Dorsally male is a more silvery-blue than the Greenish Blue (*P. saepiolus*) and quite a distinctive color compared to other Blues. The female is orange-brown similar to the Greenish Blue (*P. saepiolus*). VFW has six to eight distinct black spots and VHW is primarily whitish. Habitat: Alpine and "Canadian" zones as well as prairie and open woodlands. Host plants: Herb primrose (Family Primulaceae), alpine rock jasmine (*Androsace chamaejasme*), the Pea Family (*Fabaceae*), milk-vetches (*Astragalus* spp.), and saxifrages (*Saxifraga* spp.).

38. ARROWHEAD BLUE (*Glaucopsyche piasus*) (Plate 8; 1.125–1.375", 28.57–34.92mm) This blue is distinguished by having checkered black and white wing fringes both dorsally and ventrally. Both sexes are blue dorsally and ventrally graybrown with black spots circled in white. The HW postmedian band is composed of white arrowheads (chevrons) with the points facing inward. Habitat: Usually in mountains, forest

openings, trails, roadsides, grassy meadows, sagebrush scrub, clearings, streamsides. Host plants: Legumes (Family Fabaceae), lupines (*Lupinus* spp.), and milk-vetches (*Astragalus* spp.). In ancient Greek, psyche meant soul. Is it not a beautiful notion to think of these souls of nature flitting about on a summer's day?

39. SILVERY BLUE (*Glaucopsyche lygdamus*) (Plate 8; 1–1.25", 25.4–31.75mm) Both wings of this species have white fringes. The male is dorsally silvery blue with black margins, while the female is blackish-brown. Ventrally both sexes have a solid gray ground color and both FW and HW have a single bold row of black round spots with white trim. Habitat: Uncultivated fields, open brushlands, forest edges, meadows, roadsides. Found in a variety of elevations and cover. Host plants: Herb and shrub legumes (Family *Fabaceae*), milk-vetches (*Astragalus* spp.) and lupines (*Lupinus* spp.), showy locoweed (*Oxytropis lambertii*) and vetches (*Vicia* spp.), goldenbeans (*Thermopsis* spp.), alfalfa (*Medicago sativa*), and white sweet-clover (*Melilotus alba*).

**Hairstreaks (Subfamily Theclinae)**

In 1917, Clarence Weed noted that these species got their name "on account of the fine, hair-like markings which extend across the under surface of the hind wings." Many species also manifest delicate, hair-like tails on the hind wing. Weed described the Hairstreaks as "among the most exquisite and delicate of all our butterflies."

40. BEHR'S HAIRSTREAK (*Satyrium behrii*) (Plate 5; 1–1.25", 25–32mm) Tailless. Dorsally warm orange/brown color with broad brown borders on the margin and costa of the FW. Ventrally somewhat green base color with black submarginal dashes on FW, replaced by chevrons on HW; irregular black speckles and dashes are also present on inner two-thirds of HW. Red or orange crescent surrounded by black can be seen near bottom distal angle of HW. Habitat: Dry mountain

slopes, creeks and canyons, associated with sagebrush. Nectar: Buckwheat flowers (*Eriogonum* spp.). Host plant: Antelopebrush (*Purshia tridentata*).

41. HEDGEROW HAIRSTREAK (*Satyrium saepium*) (Plate 5; 1–1.125", 25–28mm) Small, dull brown butterfly with auburn colors dorsally and a green iridescent sheen when recently emerged; ventrally more dull brown with faint blue spots near short HW tail. Small spots may line the postmedian and/or submarginal area of both wings. Resembles the Brown Elfin (*Callophyrs augustinus*), but the Hedgerow Hairstreak (*S. saepium*) has less bicoloring of ventral wings. Habitat: Arid forests or scrub, shrubs and thickets. Nectar: Adults feed on the flowers of buckwheats (*Eriogonum* spp.) and snowbrush (*Ceanothus velutinus*). Host plant: Mountain mahogany (*Cercocarpus montanus*).

42. CALIFORNIA HAIRSTREAK (*Satyrium californica*) (Plate 5; 1–1.25", 25–32mm) Dorsally pale gray to brown-gray with a bluish sheen when recently emerged. Resembles the Sylvan Hairstreak (*S. sylvinus*) but with darker ground color and more prominent orange dusting near margins of DHW. Ventrally brown-gray with several to many orange crescents on female's HW; thin red crescent over blue patch near tail may also be present. Habitat: Brushlands, edge, and open woodlands. Nectar: Snowbrush (*Ceanothus velutinus*). Host plants: Serviceberry (*Amelanchier alnifolia*), and mountain mahogany (*Cercocarpus montanus*). Uncommon. This species occurs primarily west of the GYE.

43. CORAL HAIRSTREAK (*Satyrium titus*) (Plate 5; 1–1.25", 25–32mm) Small, brown butterfly with dark, pointed triangular wings and prominent orange spots along the VHW margin. Ventrally, the butterfly is a warm gray-black. Habitat: Meadows, brushy clearings, watercourses, and mountain canyons. Nectar: Rocky mountain bee-plant (*Cleome serrulata*) is a favorite nectar source. Host plants: Serviceberry (*Amelanchier alnifolia*) and plums and cherries (*Prunus* spp.). A site

where this species can be found in the GYE is the Lozier Hill scree slopes.

44. SOOTY HAIRSTREAK (*Satyrium fuliginosa*) (Plate 5; 1–1.25", 25–32mm) Dorsally dull gray-brown with pale fringe; HW is rounded and lacks a tail. Ventrally ash gray to dull brown; one or two rows of white ringed dark spots line submarginal FW. Spots are reduced or absent on HW. Habitat: Meadows among pine forests, dry mountainsides, plateaus, rolling grasslands and roadsides. Host plants: Lupines (*Lupinus* spp.).

45. SYLVAN HAIRSTREAK (*Satyrium sylvinus*) (Plate 5; 0.875–1.25", 22–32mm) Silver hairstreak similar to the Coral Hairstreak (*S. titus*). Dorsally it appears blue-gray with orange corners. Ventrally, it is silver with black spots surrounded by white, orange and blue spots near tail. Habitat: Foothills near rivers, mountain canyons, sometimes wet meadows, always near willows in and along drainages. Nectar: Prefers milkweed flowers (*Asclepias* spp.). Host plants: Willows (*Salix* spp.).

46. ACADIAN HAIRSTREAK (*Satyrium acadica*) (Plate 16; 1–1.2", 26–31mm) A tailed hairstreak. Ventrally gray with row of orange submarginal spots capped with black. Hindwing has postmedian row of round black spots and blue tail-spot capped with orange. The black bar above the blue tail-spot is often capped with orange. More pale than the California Hairstreak (*S. californica*). Habitat: Willows and streams. Nectar: Milkweeds (*Asclepias* spp.). Host plants: Willows (*Salix* spp.). This species is uncommon and there is some evidence that its range is retreating northward due to global warming.

47. SHERIDAN'S HAIRSTREAK (*Callophrys sheridanii*) (Plate 6; 0.75–0.875", 19–22mm) Taxonomists have assigned to the genus *Callophrys* some species that as recently as 1981 were listed under another genus, *Incisalia*. Tailless, very small green butterfly with white fringes. Dorsally it is dark grayish brown, while it is ventrally dark green, with a white postmedian line

that is fairly straight and is present on both HW and FW. Habitat: 6,000–10,000 ft. open hillsides, canyon slopes, washes, and sagebrush. Host plants: Species of the buckwheats (*Eriogonum* spp.). More common in the southern part of the GYE.

48. BRAMBLE HAIRSTREAK (*Callophrys dumetorum*) (Plate 6; 0.875–1.125", 22–28mm) Tailless, green butterfly very similar to Sheridan's Hairstreak (*C. sheridanii*). The feature that distinguishes this species from Sheridan's Hairstreak (*C. sheridanii*) is that the white postmedian line is absent or broken into faint marks. Dorsally, the male is dark gray brown; the female has prominent orange tint. Ventrally the butterfly is green with yellow shading and a grayish area at center of the FW. Habitat: Woodlands, lower mountains, sagebrush. Host plants: Wild buckwheats (*Eriogonum* spp.), such as sulphur buckwheat (*Eriogonum umbellatum*). More common in the southern part of the GYE.

49. HOARY ELFIN (*Callophrys polios*) (Plate 6; 0.75–1", 19–25mm) Small, brown-colored with a scalloped HW, lobe at bottom inner angle of HW small, fringes dark at vein ends. Dorsally it is grayish brown. Ventrally the outer margin of FW is narrowly frosty gray, resembling tree bark; with an undulating postmedian line black inwardly, white outwardly. HW dark at base, outer half usually frosty gray and scalloped with postmedian line of brown spots. Habitat: Dry open rocky areas, generally above 8,000 ft. Host plants: Shrubby members of the Heath Family (Ericaceae) including common bearberry (*Arctostaphylos uva-ursi*). Uncommon; range is primarily to the north of the GYE.

50. BROWN ELFIN (*Callophrys augustinus*) (Plate 6; 0.75–1.125", 19–28mm) Dull copper brown and very similar to the Hedgerow Hairstreak (*Satyrium saepium*). However, it is less patterned and more two-toned on the ventral side. Ventrally it is chocolate brown, with the outer half of the wings purplish, light brown, or mahogany. Wing margins are sometimes black

and white checkered. HW margins are lightly scalloped. Habitat: Open woodland meadows, bogs, and shrubby forest margins. Nectar: Usually from the Heath Family (Ericaceae), especially common bearberry (*Arctostaphylos uva-ursi*). Host plants: Shrubs, trees, vines and herbs in the Heath Family (Ericaceae): common bearberry (*Arctostaphylos uva-ursi*) and huckleberries (*Vaccinium* spp.). This species is most likely to be observed in the northern GYE.

51. JUNIPER HAIRSTREAK (*Callophrys gryneus*) (Plate 6; 1", 25mm) As the name implies, this butterfly is distinctly green on the ventral side, but warm brown on the dorsal side, and it is often found near junipers (*Juniperus* spp.). It has a relatively straight white postmedian line extending from VFW to VHW; several submarginal black spots, and one orange spot encased in black may be seen on the lower VHW. Habitat: Dry or rocky open areas. Food: Species of junipers (*Juniperus* spp.). Host plants: Same as adult food sources. This species is most likely to be observed in the southern GYE.

52. WESTERN PINE ELFIN (*Callophrys eryphon*) (Plate 6; 0.75–1.25", 19–32mm) This species is often found on woodland margins perched on lodgepole pine saplings. Dorsally it is chocolate brown; while ventrally it has a brown to red bark pattern with inward pointing chevrons of dark brown on margin and a crooked white stripe through both wings. It is quite cryptic sitting on a tree. Habitat: Canyon bottoms and streamside glades, spruce bogs, meadows in pine forests. Nectar: Alpine pussytoes (*Antennaria alpina*), alder-leaved buckthorn (*Rhamnus alnifolia*), wild roses (*Rosa* spp.), and lupines (*Lupinus* spp.). Host plants: Lodgepole pine (*Pinus contorta*) and ponderosa pine (*Pinus ponderosa*).

53. THICKET HAIRSTREAK (*Callophrys spinetorum*) (Plate 6; 1–1.25", 25–32mm) Navy blue hairstreak with white edges and two small tails per HW. Ventrally, the species is reddish brown with obvious black-edged white postmedian line forming a "w" near HW tails; series of black spots can be seen on sub-

marginal HW. Habitat: Coniferous forests or woodlands, usually in clearings or small canyons. Nectar: Buckwheats (*Eriogonum* spp.) and composites. Host plants: Species of dwarf mistletoes (*Arceuthobium* spp.) that parasitize conifers, especially pines and firs.

## Coppers (Subfamily Lycaeninae)

Most of these species display shades of coppery-brown on the upper wing surfaces. To keep us all attentive, however, a very few blue-colored butterflies have been classified as coppers, and a very few copper-colored ones are organized with the blues!

54. RUDDY COPPER (*Lycaena rubidus*) (Plate 6M/16F; 1.125–1.25", 28–32mm) This bright copper butterfly is relatively easy to identify, especially if the male is observed. The only species that a male might be confused with is the Lustrous Copper (*L. cupreus*), which is brighter orange and smaller than the Ruddy Copper (*L. rubidus*). The female is a dull orange-brown color. Both sexes show black spots on DFW. Ventrally very white with black spots on FW; HW generally without markings. Habitat: Found at moderate to high elevations in open dry areas and sagebrush stands near meadows or streams. Nectar: Buckwheats (*Eriogonum* spp.), common rabbitbrush (*Chrysothamnus nauseosus*), and shrubby cinquefoil (*Pentaphylloides floribunda*). Host plants: Docks (*Rumex* spp.).

55. BRONZE COPPER (*Lycaena hyllus*) (Plate 16; 1.25–1.625", 32–41mm) Dorsally dark copper-brown with violet hue on FW, orange or yellow HW margin. The ventral side of the butterfly is most distinctive. The VFW is orange with black spots, while the VHW is white with small black spots and a fiery orange margin. Habitat: Moist areas, such as grassy and sedgy margins of wet meadows, swamps, and small streams. Seldom visits flowers. Host plants: Docks (*Rumex* spp.) and pondweeds (*Potamogeton* spp.). The range of this species is

primarily to the northeast, but it may be seen in wet meadows of the GYE.

56. PURPLISH COPPER (*Lycaena helloides*) (Plate 7; 0.94–1.31", 24–33mm) Male and female are both dorsally a dull copper brown, but male has a purplish iridescence. Ventrally the HW is a dull pinkish tan to grayish tan, with a distinctive scalloped orange-red submarginal line. Habitat: Wide variety, often in conjunction with moist areas. Host plants: Docks (*Rumex* spp.), and knotweeds (*Polygonum* spp.).

57. MARIPOSA COPPER (*Lycaena mariposa*) (Plate 7; 1.06–1.25", 27–32mm) As compared to the Purplish Copper (*L. helloides*), this butterfly is much more dull and woody colored. Dorsally the male is brown with a purplish iridescence, whereas the female is much more orange and brown. Ventrally they both exhibit a brownish gray woody pattern. Habitat: Mountains below timberline, moist areas. Host plants: Buckwheat Family (Polygonaceae) including curled dock (*Rumex crispus*).

58. LILAC-BORDERED COPPER (*Lycaena nivalis*) (Plate 7; 1–1.325", 25–34mm) This butterfly appears very similar to the Purplish Copper (*L. helloides*) dorsally, but its ventral side has the distinctive characteristics. Dorsally the male is coppery brown, with lilac reflections and a moderate dusky border. The submarginal line on the HW is orange, and irregular with two to four small, dark spots at margin. The female is usually dull orange with thicker black wing borders and larger black spots on the FW spots. Ventrally both sexes have a FW which is yellowish-white and heavily spotted, whereas the VHW is pinkish gray with lilac edges and a fine submarginal orange markings. Habitat: Mountain meadows, forest openings, streamsides, sagebrush flats, alpine fell fields. Host plants: Buckwheat Family (Polygonaceae) including mountain knotweed (*Polygonum douglasii*).

59. LUSTROUS COPPER (*Lycaena cupreus*) (Plate 7; 1–1.25", 25–30mm) This is the most brilliantly colored orange copper

butterfly. Dorsally it is an iridescent brilliant reddish copper with dark brown to black spotting. Males are somewhat more brilliantly colored and females more spotted dorsally. Ventrally, the FW is orange or copper, HW is whitish-yellow. Habitat: Flowery meadows, rocky streambeds and trenches, talus slopes. Host plants: Buckwheat Family (Polygonaceae): alpine sorrel (*Rumex paucifolius*), sheep sorrel (*R. acetosella*), green sorrel (*R. acetosa*), mountain sorrel (*Oxyria digyna*).

60. BLUE COPPER (*Lycaena heteronea*) (Plate 7; 1–1.32", 25–33mm) This large blue Lycaenid is distinguished by its prominent veins and very white ventral side with very few markings. The female has similar markings on the ventral side but is a dull brown dorsally. Habitat: Low to middle elevation mountain canyons, sagelands, and flowery river flats and plateaus. Nectar: Buckwheats (*Eriogonum* spp.). Host plants: Buckwheat Family (Polygonaceae) including sulphur buckwheat (*Eriogonum umbellatum*).

61. AMERICAN COPPER (*Lycaena phlaeas*) (Plate 7; 0.875–1.125", 22–28mm) Dorsally this species is bi-colored, with orange FW, brown HW, and orange border to HW. Ventrally it is also bi-colored with a silver-gray HW and more orange scaling on the FW. Habitat: Barren ground, talus slopes, and fell fields. Nectar: Mountain sorrel (*Oxyria digyna*). Host plants: Buckwheats (Family Polygonaceae) including sheep sorrel (*Rumex acetosella*), curled dock (*R. crispus*), green sorrel (*R. acetosa*), mountain sorrel (*Oxyria digyna*).

62. EDITH'S COPPER (*Lycaena editha*) (Plate 16; .88–1.25", 22–30mm) This species is most easily distinguished by its "reptilian" coloration and pattern on the VHW. Dorsally it is taupe. Ventrally, it is buff with black spots on the FW. Orange-black spots cover most of the HW and it is edged in white chevrons. Habitat: Dry slopes, sagebrush flats, and dry riverbeds. Nectar: Docks (*Rumex* spp.) or milkweeds (*Asclepias* spp.). Host plants: Buckwheats (Family Polygonaceae),

including curled dock (*Rumex crispus*), sheep sorrel (*R. acetosella*), alpine sorrel (*R. paucifolius*), willow dock (*R. salicifolius*), and western dock (*R. aquaticus*).

63. GREAT GRAY COPPER (*Lycaena dione*) (Plate 7; .94–1.5", 24–38mm) This name aptly describes the largest of the Lycaenids in the GYE. This large gray copper has submarginal orange bands on the DHW and VHW. The dorsal side is a darker gray while the ventral side is more of a whitish-gray with black spots. Habitat: Parklands, prairies, and foothills and often found near moist areas such as ponds, streams, and rivers. Host plants: Docks and sorrels (*Rumex* spp.). This species is more common in more eastern parts of the U.S., but it may be found in the northern part of the GYE.

**BRUSHFOOTED BUTTERFLIES:
INCLUDING FRITILLARIES, [GREATER AND
LESSER FRITILLARIES], TRUE BRUSHFOOTS
[CHECKERSPOTS AND CRESCENTS, ANGLEWINGS,
TORTOISESHELLS, AND LADIES], ADMIRALS,
SATYRS, AND MONARCHS (FAMILY NYMPHALIDAE)**

The Nymphalidae are called brushfooted butterflies because the front legs are greatly reduced (in both sexes, but especially in males) to less than half the normal size in most species. These small legs are covered with hair, thus appearing like a brush. This family is a very diverse grouping, includes many species, and has been regarded as cosmopolitan. The traditional sense of this word is "belonging to all parts of the world," or "free from national prejudices, a citizen of the world," agreeing with the botanical or zoological sense of cosmopolitan as "widely distributed over the globe." Along with the Lycaenids, the Nymphalidae comprise many of the species you'll find in the Yellowstone. Of 185 North American species, forty-one are regularly found in the ecosystem. Some species of this family migrate, including the Painted Lady

(*Vanessa cardui*). Many are medium to large in size, but the Crescents include some smaller species. They range from bright to dull colored. Veins of FW not swollen at base except in a few genera. HW discal cell usually open; antennae finely scaled. Here we have also continued to use some of the older subdivisions of larger subfamilies for ease of identification (e.g., Fritillaries are separated into Greater and Lesser Fritillaries; and True Brushfoots are separated into Checkerspots and Crescents, Anglewings, Tortoiseshells, and Ladies).

## Fritillaries (Subfamily Heliconiinae)

### Greater Fritillaries (*genus* Speyeria)

Of fourteen North American species, ten show up in the Yellowstone. They are large in size, generally display hues of orange with distinctive dark bands, spangles, and spots. Interesting to note is that this group seems to avoid laying eggs on the caterpillar's food plant. They lay their eggs in grasses, where caterpillars hatch, overwinter, then in the spring make their way to violets. These species can be difficult to separate without a good view, especially of the ventral hindwings. The color of the VHW spots and/or the color of the VHW margins can be a good indicator. In some cases, capture is necessary to distinguish similar species, but a good pair of binoculars and a steady hand is an excellent alternative after some careful study and practice.

64. APHRODITE FRITILLARY (*Speyeria aphrodite*) (Plate 12; 2.5–3", 63.5–76.2mm) Dorsally male is orange-brown with dark markings evenly spaced. Wing bases darkened slightly or not at all. Female similar, but larger and paler. VHW disc cinnamon brown to deep red-brown with almost no cream submarginal band. Spots large, well silvered. Habitat: Moist meadows, streamsides, old fields, mountain slopes, and prairies. Host plants: Violets (Family Violaceae) including yellow montane violet (*Viola nuttallii*), and northern bog violet (*V. nephrophylla*). Uncommon in the GYE, and

more likely to be observed in the northern part of the ecosystem.

65. GREAT SPANGLED FRITILLARY (*Speyeria cybele*) (Plate 12; 2.5–3.5", 63.5–88.9mm) One of the largest *Speyeria* in the region, but infrequently observed. The male is generally orange and black dorsally, whereas the female has dark wing bases, and the outer half of the wings lighter. VHW disc is brown, with a wide and yellowish submarginal band. All spots large and well silvered. Habitat: Meadows, streamsides, aspen groves, open woodland, prairies, roadsides. Host plants: Violets (Family Violaceae) such as early blue violet (*Viola adunca*) and Canada violet (*V. canadensis*).

66. HESPERIS ATLANTIS FRITILLARY (*Speyeria atlantis hesperis*) (Plate 11; 2–2.75", 50.8–69.85mm) Dorsally orange and black; ventrally deep burgundy brown with creme or silvered spots. No lavender tint. VHW submarginal band is cream colored and narrower than the Hydaspe Fritillary (*S. hydaspe*). Habitat: Variable, but tends to be woody. Host plants: Violets (Family Violaceae), including early blue violet (*Viola adunca*), Canada violet (*V. canadensis*), northern bog violet (*V. nephrophylla*) and yellow montane violet (*V. nuttallii*).

67. HYDASPE FRITILLARY (*Speyeria hydaspe*) (Plate 11; 2–2.5", 50.8–63.5mm) Dorsally bright orange-brown; dark markings heavy. Wing bases usually very dark. Ventrally brick red with lavender tint. Creme-colored (not silvered) spots edged with black. VHW submarginal band is a warm brownish-brick color and wider than the Hesperis Atlantis Fritillary (*S. atlantis hesperis*). Habitat: Mountain meadows, forest openings. Host plants: Violets (Family Violaceae) including stream violet (*Viola glabella*), round-leaved yellow violet (*V. orbiculata*), yellow montane violet (*V. nuttallii*), and early blue violet (*V. adunca*).

68. CALLIPPE FRITILLARY (*Speyeria callippe*) (Plate 11; 2–2.5", 50.8–63.5mm) Major distinguishing characteristic is that this is the most green of the *Speyeria* on VHW discal cell.

Edwards' Fritillary (*S. edwardsii*) is also green, but is more of a gray-green on the VHW and is usually larger. VHW spots large, usually silvered. Silver submarginal spots triangular, with greenish shading. Dorsally bright red-brown to light tawny, depending on subspecies. Females are lighter than males dorsally. Usually spangled. Dark markings evenly spaced, giving a distinctive checkered appearance. Habitat: Variable. Host plant: Yellow montane violet (*Viola nuttallii*).

69. ZERENE FRITILLARY (*Speyeria zerene*) (Plate 11; 2.15–2.75", 54.6–69.85mm) FW margin is slightly concave. Dorsally bright red-brown to tawny (not smoky), median line usually wide and dark. VFW submarginal spots are large and silvered. VHW is bi-colored with three upper spots in median band that are all separate; second spot is round and larger, third spot smaller, slanted away from second. VHW submarginal area is tan like the Hesperis Atlantis Fritillary (*S. atlantis hesperis*). Lavender tint. Host plants: Violets (Family Violaceae), including early blue violet (*Viola adunca*) and yellow montane violet (*V. nuttallii*).

70. EDWARDS' FRITILLARY (*Speyeria edwardsii*) (Plate 11; 2.5–2.75", 63.5–69.85mm) One of the larger and more colorful of the Rocky Mountain butterflies, but not often seen in the GYE. Dorsally bright tawny, spangled. Dark markings moderate, evenly spaced; bold black border well-marked with chevrons that point inward; spots inside border are lighter in color than many other *Speyeria* species. Ventrally dull gray-green. VHW spots large, brilliantly silvered, oval shaped, and slightly transparent. Habitat: Meadows, fields, glades, roadsides; seldom above 10,000 ft. Host plants: Violets (Family Violaceae) including yellow montane violet (*Viola nuttallii*), early blue violet (*V. adunca*). *Speyeria edwardsii* was named for naturalist William Henry Edwards. Accounts of collecting specimens up the Amazon River inspired Alfred Russell Wallace and Henry Walter Bates to embark on their explorations. Although Edwards did not embark for the American West until 1894, with son-in-law Theodore L. Mead, he named

many western butterflies. Trained in law and occupied with business interests, Edwards nonetheless found time to engage in his passion for butterflies, writing the beautifully illustrated three-volume *Butterflies of North America* (1868–1897).

71. GREAT BASIN FRITILLARY (*Speyeria egleis*) (Plate 11; 1.75–2.375", 44.45–60.33mm) Brownish-green tint to both dorsal and ventral sides; especially prominent ventrally. Similar to the Zerene Fritillary (*S. zerene*), but smaller. Dorsally smoky coloration with dark suffusion in basal half of orange-brown wings. Ventrally spots small, separate, with narrow dark edges inwardly and heavy dark shading outwardly. Spots usually silvered, but not always. Habitat: Transition to Canadian zone, forest openings but usually on exposed, rocky ridges. Host plants: Violets (Family Violaceae) including early blue violet (*Viola adunca*), and yellow montane violet (*V. nuttallii*). Type locality at Elkhorn ranch, MT. Uncommon, but may be observed in the southern GYE.

72. CORONIS FRITILLARY (*Speyeria coronis*) (Plate 11; 2.5–2.75", 63.5–69.85mm) Dorsally dull tawny to bright reddish brown. Similar to the Zerene Fritillary (*S. zerene*), but larger. Wing bases little darkened, wing borders moderately dark. Ventrally mottled brown and buffy. Submarginal band narrow, VHW spots are triangular, large and silvered, with brown capping. Habitat: Various, meadows, openings, mountain slopes, foothills, and sagebrush scrub. Food: Adults sip flower nectar and occasionally mud. Host plant: Yellow montane violet (*Viola nuttallii*). Low likelihood of observing in GYE.

73. MORMON FRITILLARY (*Speyeria mormonia*) (Plate 11; 1.5–2.175", 38.1–55.24mm) One of the smallest and most common *Speyeria* in the GYE. Dorsally tawny to bright orange-brown. Dark markings narrow, well separated. VHW light greenish tint and highly variable in spot coloration (from cream to silver). Habitat: Alpine meadows and fell-fields.

Host plants: Violets (Family Violaceae) such as yellow montane violet (*Viola nuttallii*), northern bog violet (*V. nephrophylla*), and early blue violet (*V. adunca*).

## *Lesser Fritillaries (genus* Boloria*)*

Smaller than the greater fritillaries, these may be hard to get a good look at, because they are so very busy with the business of being a butterfly. They too are best identified after viewing the ventral patterning and coloration but are somewhat easier to separate than the greater fritillaries.

74. FREIJA FRITILLARY (*Boloria freija*) (Plate 16; 1.25–1.5", 32–39mm) Dorsally orange and black as in most fritillaries. The distinguishing characteristic is the VHW with median zigzag black line and arrowhead-shaped white spots in the center of the wing and at the wing margins. Habitat: Subalpine willow bogs. Host plants: Heath Family (Ericaceae).

75. FRIGGA FRITILLARY (*Boloria Frigga*) (Plate 12; 1.49–1.6", 38–41mm) This species is only seen in wet willow bogs. Dorsally dull orange very dark overscaling. Borders usually wide and dark. Ventrally dark with a band of buffy spots. Distinguishing character is the pearly gray coastal bar on VHW. Habitat: Willow bogs and tundra. Host plants: Mostly shrubs of the Willow Family (Salicaceae).

76. MEADOW FRITILLARY (*Boloria bellona*) (Plate 12; 1.625–1.75", 41.3–44.45mm) Dorsally orange; markings very evenly spaced on basal half of wings, small and widely spaced on outer half. Distinguished by the ventrally purplish brown markings on FW apex and on all of HW which are blurred on VHW, resembling a smeared watercolor painting. Habitat: Meadows, streamsides, open woodland. Host plants: Violets (Family Violaceae) including stream violet (*Viola glabella*), and northern bog violet (*V. nephrophylla*). This species is on the edge of its range in the GYE and is more likely to be observed farther north.

77. RELICT FRITILLARY (*Boloria kriemhild*) (Plate 12; 1.375–1.75", 34–44mm) Dorsally bright orange-brown; dark markings small, widely spaced. Wing bases have little dark suffusion. VHW with yellow spots outlined in brown. DHW submarginal line narrow, consisting of flat brown chevrons pointing outward. Habitat: Mountain meadows, streamsides, forest edges and openings. Host plants: Violets (Family Violaceae). This species, like the Gillett's Checkerspot and Hayden's Ringlet, is a relict in the sense that its closest relatives live in Eurasia. These three species share a similar range; the central Rocky Mountains, from southwest Montana to Northeast Utah.

78. SILVER-BORDERED FRITILLARY (*Boloria selene*) (Plate 12; 1.3–1.8", 34–47mm) Dorsally light orange brown; dark markings heaviest at border and near bases. Postmarginal band has one row of small black spots. Ventrally light spots brightly silvered; marginal silver spots complete. Habitat: Meadows, bogs, forest openings, marshes in mountain areas. Host plants: Violets (Family Violaceae).

79. BOG FRITILLARY (*Boloria Eunomia*) (Plate 12; 1.3–1.6", 32–42mm) Dull orange with dark scaling dorsally at wing bases. Distinguished by the VHW row of white-centered postmedian circles outlined in black, the large marginal spots, and the white median cell spot in the inner margin of the VHW, which is convex outwardly. Habitat: Wetlands, seeps, and bogs. Host plants: Willows (*Salix* spp.), bistorts (*Polygonum* spp.), and violets (*Viola* spp.).

80. ARCTIC FRITILLARY (*Boloria chariclea*) (Plate 12; 1.2–1.7", 32–44mm) Dorsally black bars or dots on dark orange. Large black submarginal dots closely connected. Brown chevrons point inward. Ventrally FW like dorsal, HW mottled rust and purple with marginal white spots. Habitat: Moist bogs, wet places and along trails. Host plants: Herb and shrub willows (Family Salicaceae); Netted willow (*Salix reticulata*); buckwheats (Family Polygonaceae); American bistort (*Polygonum*

*bistortoides*), alpine bistort (*P. viviparum*); violets (Family Violaceae): early blue violet (*Viola adunca*); Oviposition on huckleberries (*Vaccinium* spp.).

## True Brushfoots (Subfamily Nymphalinae)

*Checkerspots and Crescents*

Crescents are named for the pattern found on the VHW near the wing margins. Checkerspots look just as their name implies, wings full of tiny checkered spots, mostly in white, orange, and black. Watch for subtle variations between species and differences between sexes in some species.

81. MYLITTA CRESCENT (*Phyciodes mylitta*) (Plate 10; 1–1.25", 26–37mm) Of all the Crescents, this species has the least amount of dorsal dark markings. Dorsally bright orange; dark markings narrow, evenly spaced. No heavy black spots. Ventrally no black spots on FW. Rusty brown markings on HW moderate to well developed. Habitat: Fields, meadows, fencerows, roadsides, roads, parks, vacant lots. Host plants: Thistles (*Cirsium* spp.). Uncommon in the GYE; primary range is farther west.

82. FIELD CRESCENT (*Phyciodes campestris*) (Plate 10; 94–1.5", 24–39mm) Antennal knobs brown. Dorsally dark with stained glass pattern of orange and black. Ventrally extremely light in coloration compared to other *Phyciodes* species. Habitat: Open areas and glades, often near streams. Host plants: Aster Family (Asteraceae), fleabanes (*Erigeron* spp.).

83. NORTHERN CRESCENT (*Phyciodes selenis*) (Plate 10; 1.25–1.7", 32–43mm) Dorsally distinguished by larger areas of orange and black markings than the Field Crescent (*P. campestris*). If one looks closely, especially in the male, you may imagine a rabbit in the DFW (nose is pointed towards wing margin). Ventrally yellowish orange and orangish brown patches, again with fewer dark markings. Row of light inward pointing chevrons. Habitat: Open meadows; also

along streams. Nectar: Aster Family (Asteraceae). Host plants: Aster Family (Asteraceae).

84. PALE CRESCENT (*Phyciodes pallida*) (Plate 10; 1.2–1.5", 30–39mm) Dorsally irregular black and orange patterns, ventrally hindwing has submarginal off-white spots. Larger than the Mylitta Crescent (*P. mylitta*). VFW has square black patch in center of trailing margin. Habitat: Gullies and streams in foothills and mountains. Host plants: Thistles (*Cirsium* spp.).

85. SAGEBRUSH CHECKERSPOT (*Chlosyne acastus*) (Plate 13; 1.2–1.5", 31–39mm) Dorsally orange with black bands. VFW mottled orange with white bands. HW alternating bands of reddish-brown and pearly white spots and crescents (rather than cream or yellow as in the Northern Checkerspot [*C. palla*]). Habitat: Pine woodlands, canyons in lower elevations, mountains. Host plants: Herb and shrub asters (Family Asteraceae).

86. NORTHERN CHECKERSPOT (*Chlosyne Palla*) (Plate 13; 1.25–1.625", 31.7–41.27mm) Dorsally dark orange with black lines and patches. Ventrally FW orange with marginal black-bordered yellowish-cream median bands; VHW with yellow crescent row next to red margin. Light patches are cream-yellow rather than white as in the Sagebrush Checkerspot (*C. acastus*). Habitat: Mountain clearings and valleys, sagebrush canyons, valleys with aspen. Host plants: Aster Family (Asteraceae); common rabbitbrush (*Chrysothamnus nauseosus*), showy fleabane (*Erigeron speciosus*), arrow-leaved groundsel (*Senecio triangularis*).

87. GORGONE CHECKERSPOT (*Chlosyne gorgone*) (Plate 13; 1.1–1.4", 28–37mm) Dorsally background blackish; spots and bands orange-brown. Median band complete. FW and HW have a small orange chevron in outer edge. Ventrally has a zigzag pattern of alternating brown and white bars and scallops. Habitat: Plains, foothills, and brushlands to 10,000 ft. Nectar: Various members of the Sunflower Family. Host plants: Herb and shrub-like asters (Family Asteraceae) includ-

ing common sunflower (*Helianthus annuus*) and goldeneye (*Heliomeris multiflora*).

88. EDITH'S CHECKERSPOT (*Euphydryas editha*) (Plate 13; 1–1.7", 26–43mm) Smaller and more orange colored dorsally (as opposed to black) than the Variable Checkerspot (*E. chalcedona*). DFW distal edge forms almost straight line. Wings short and rounded. Dorsally orange with black outlined proximal cream bands. Ventrally much more cream-colored with less black. Habitat: Evergreen forests, sagebrush hills, alpine tundra, ridge tops. Host plants: Usually annual herbs including the Figwort Family (Scrophulariaceae): Indian paintbrushes (*Castelleja* spp.), elephant's heads and louseworts (*Pedicularis* spp.), penstemons (*Penstemon* spp.); also members of the Valerian (Valerianaceae), plantain (Plantaginaceae), and honeysuckle (Caprifoliaceae) families.

89. VARIABLE CHECKERSPOT (*Euphydryas chalcedona*) (Plate 13; 1.13–2", 28–51mm) Aptly named for the variability in wing color patterns within the species. Similar to Edith's Checkerspot (*E. editha*), but larger with more black and less orange dorsally. Dorsally black with cream colored dots on black background. Ventrally with reddish-orange and cream spots. Habitat: Tundra and ridges, pine forests, grasslands with aspen groves, mountain meadows, and sagelands. Host plants: Figwort Family (Scrophulariaceae): Indian paintbrushes (*Castelleja* spp.), penstemons (*Penstemon* spp.), elephant's heads and louseworts (*Pedicularis* spp.), with occasional species of other genera; Valerian Family (Valerianaceae); Broomrape Family (Orobanchaceae) such as clustered broomrape (*Orobanche fasciculata*); Plantain Family (Plantaginaceae) including plantagos (*Plantago* spp.); Honeysuckle Family (Caprifoliaceae) such as honeysuckles (*Lonicera* spp.), snowberries (*Symphoricarpos* spp.), and occasionally species from other families.

90. GILLETT'S CHECKERSPOT (*Euphydryas gillettii*) (Plate 13; 1.375–1.75", 35–44mm) Distinguished by broad reddish-orange

submarginal band on DFW and DHW. This species' common name was recently updated from Gillette's to Gillett's in order to reflect the historical benefactor of the scientist that named this butterfly. Habitat: Moist clearings among lodgepole pine forest and mountain meadows. F/HWs form rounded half oval. Host plant: Black twinberry (*Lonicera involucrata*). Note that this species is very rare in the ecosystem and if observed, should not be collected.

**Anglewings, Tortoiseshells, and Ladies**

The Anglewings (genus *Polygonia*), Tortoiseshells (genus *Nymphalis*), and Ladies (genus *Vanessa*) have several similar traits, including wing shape, coloration, and behavior. We're tempted to think Anglewings got their name from the sharp angles their wings display. Indeed, the first characteristic Holland noted was "the more or less deeply excavated inner and outer margins of the forewings," and a "tail like projection of the hind wings"(but not as pronounced as a swallowtail). Comstock wrote that the Anglewings could be distinguished by their hairy eyes, while Weed noted three ridges on the hairless portion of the antenna club (did you bring your hand-lens?). In the field, what's most noticeable are the uneven trailing wing margins. They appear deeply scalloped, perhaps appearing tattered or like a modernist expression when compared to other butterfly wings. When they alight and close their wings, Anglewings and Tortoiseshells disappear amongst dead leaves or on tree bark, perfectly disguised. All three groups are frequently found along forested trailsides. The Anglewings and Tortoiseshells rarely nectar, but prefer food in the form of rotten fruit, animal scat, or carrion. Adult Anglewings and Tortoiseshells overwinter in the adult form in hollow trees and are some of the first butterflies to come out on a warm spring day.

*Anglewings (genus* Polygonia*)*

91. HOARY COMMA (*Polygonia gracilis*) (Plate 10; 1.75–2.175", 44.45–55.25mm) Dorsally bright tawny. HW bor-

der diffuse. Light submarginal spots shaped like arrowheads, pointing inward; spots usually have small dark centers. The distinguishing characteristic of this Nymphalid is the ventrally gray coloration. Area at base dark; outer area much lighter, with tiny dark etchings. Silver cell spot on VHW thin; curved or L-shaped. Habitat: Forests, brushlands, and streamside woodland in mountain areas. Host plant: Wax currant (*Ribes cereum*).

92. OREAS COMMA (*Polygonia oreas*) (Plate 10; 1.75–2", 44–52mm). Dorsally HW is dark with submarginal yellow-orange spots. Ventrally gray to gray-brown or black with very little contrast between basal and outer portions. Habitat: Wooded streams, coniferous forests, open parklands. Host plants: Gooseberries and currants (*Ribes* spp.).

93. SATYR COMMA (*Polygonia satyrus*) (Plate 10; 1.75–2.25", 44.45–57.15mm) Dorsally bright tawny to golden. Two postmedian black spots on FW, the inner spot smaller. HW has very little brown shading, a narrow border, and light spots near margin. Ventrally banded golden and dark brown. Habitat: Moist valleys, streamsides, and fencerows; where nettle grows. Host plants: Nettle Family (Urticaceae) including stinging nettle (*Urtica dioica*).

94. GREEN COMMA (*Polygonia faunus*) (Plate 10; 1.75–2.175", 44.45–55.24mm) Dorsally deep reddish brown, with heavy dark markings. Wide dark borders often cover about half of wing surface. Submarginal spots on DHW small but distinct. Ventrally dark, heavily mottled; outer third has many greenish spots. Silver spot on VHW cell L-shaped. Habitat: Forest or canyons. Host plants: Alders (*Alnus* spp.), willows (*Salix* spp.), and northern gooseberry (*Ribes oxyacanthoides*).

*Tortoiseshells (genus* Nymphalis*)*

95. MILBERT'S TORTOISESHELL (*Nymphalis milberti*) (Plate 9; 1.675–2", 42.54–50.8mm) Dorsally blackish-brown with a

distinctive orange-yellow band positioned vertically across FW and HW. Ventrally wood-brown, with darker wing bases. Habitat: Fields, moist brushlands, streamsides, mountain passes. Host plant: Nettles (*Urtica* spp.).

96. CALIFORNIA TORTOISESHELL (*Nymphalis californica*) (Plate 9; 1.25–2.25", 31.75–57.15mm) Similar to the Compton Tortoiseshell (*N. vaualbum*), but without white spots dorsally. Habitat: Brushland, open woodland, forest edges, clearings. Host plants: Snowbrush (*Ceanothus velutinus*).

97. COMPTON TORTOISESHELL (*Nymphalis vaualbum*) (Plate 9; 2.5–2.9", 63.5–73.0mm) Dorsally orange-brown; wing bases darker brown. Larger tortoiseshell with single white spot on DFW and DHW costal margins. Ventrally marbled gray and brown, wing bases and borders darker. VHW has small white V at outer end of cell. Habitat: Usually deciduous woodland. Host plants: Birches (*Betula* spp.), willows (*Salix* spp.), aspens and cottonwoods (*Populus* spp.). Uncommon in GYE; range is primarily to the northwest.

98. MOURNING CLOAK (*Nymphalis antiopa*) (Plate 9; 2.25–3", 57.15–76.2mm) Largest Nymphalid and one of the first butterflies to be observed in the spring. Dorsally a velvety dark purplish-brown or maroon with yellow wing borders, ventrally dark brown with lighter wing margins. Habitat: Woodlands, streamsides, and parks. Host plants: Willows (*Salix* spp.), poplars and cottonwoods (*Populus* spp.).

*Ladies*

Not a subfamily, just more species of the true brushfoots, but how beautiful is the genus *Vanessa*.

99. PAINTED LADY (*Vanessa cardui*) (Plate 9; 2–2.5", 50.8–63.5mm). Dorsally, the ground color is pinkish-tawny. Wing bases are heavily clouded with brown. Dorsally very similar to the West Coast Lady (*V. annabella*) but with a white FW costal patch (rather than orange in the West Coast Lady

[*V. annabella*]). Ventrally, the pattern is complex, with four submarginal spots on VHW. Habitat: General. Host plants: Extremely broad, including thistles (*Cirsium* spp.), mallows (Family Malvaceae) and peas (Family Fabaceae). This broadranging species is known for its long migrations and large population sizes in some years. It is known as the Painted Lady, the Thistle Butterfly and the Cosmopolite. One of its important host plants is the thistle. Because this host plant is widely distributed, so is the butterfly. This species has been known as the most "cosmopolitan" of its relatives. In *Butterflies Worth Knowing* (1917), Clarence Weed called the Painted Lady (*V. cardui*) "remarkable for its powers of flight," noting it had been found far out at sea. The Painted Lady, said Weed, sometimes will congregate and migrate in a swarm. In 1879, one of these swarms reportedly migrated from Africa to Europe. In 1925, scientists still did not know where this species spent the winter. We now know that it goes to sites in southwestern U.S., southern Florida, and Mexico. Adults hibernate in mild winters or in southern sites.

100. WEST COAST LADY (*Vanessa annabella*) (Plate 9; 1.5–2", 38.1–50.8mm) Much less common than the Painted Lady (*V. cardui*). Dorsally very similar to the Painted Lady (*V. cardui*) but with an orange FW costal patch (rather than white in the Painted Lady (*V. cardui*)) and a squared-off FW tip. Ventrally also similar to the Painted Lady (*V. cardui*) but with smaller eyespots. Habitat: Canals, fields, and slopes. Host plants: Mallows (Family Malvaceae) and nettles (Family Urticaceae).

101. RED ADMIRAL (*Vanessa atalanta*) (Plate 9; 1.9–2.5", 48–65mm) Dorsally dark brown, orange bottom edges, with a little blue in the HW corners. Striking reddish-orange bands cross FWs in a diagonal pattern and white spotting on FW corners. Ventrally very colorful, FW bands appear rosier. Habitat: Forest margins and glades, rivers, meadows, open woods and clearings. Food: Sap, fruit, dung, and flower nectar. Host plants: Nettles (Family Urticaceae). The male of this species is territorial, especially in the late afternoon.

## Admirals (Subfamily Limenitidinae)

102. WEIDEMEYER'S ADMIRAL (*Limenitis weidemeyerii*) (Plate 9; 2.25–3", 57.15–76.2mm) Dorsally black, with a white median band, white spots below apex, and submarginal band of small white dots. Ventrally dark crosslines between veins at bases of HW. Postmedian band with reddish spots or crescents; submarginal and marginal crescents greenish or bluish. Habitat: Deciduous forest in mountain areas; streamsides and edges of coniferous forest. Host plants: Trees and shrubs of the Willow Family (Salicaceae): willows (*Salix* spp.), trembling aspen (*Populus tremuloides*), narrow-leaved cottonwood (*P. angustifolia*); the Rose Family (Rosaceae) including chokecherry (*Prunus virginiana*), serviceberry (*Amelanchier alnifolia*) and many oceanspray (*Holodiscus* spp.).

103. VICEROY (*Limenitis archippus*) (Plate 9; 2.25–3", 58–76mm) Mimic of the Monarch. Dorsally orange with postmedian black line on HW and a single row of white spots on black marginal bands. Habitat: Rivers and streams near forests, lake edges, and wetlands. Host plant: Willows (*Salix* spp.).

## Satyrs (Subfamily Satyrinae)

Of forty-six North American species, fifteen species of this Nymphalid family visit the GYE. Often characterized by slender abdomens and comparatively large wings that are chiefly shades of brown, and decorated by conspicuous eyespots. Small to medium-sized, Satyrs are usually brown or some nondescript shade of orange, but can also manifest whitish shades, tan, gray, brown, or black. Antennae are short and weakly clubbed. Front legs are reduced. One to three main FW veins swollen at the base in most species carry hearing organs. Flight usually jerky and bouncing, perhaps due to slow wingbeats. Satyrs are not known as powerful flyers. *Erebia* can lack the hopping motion of other Satyrs, as it flutters contentedly along. Satyrs may take refuge in grass or shrubbery if disturbed. Several of the Alpines (Theano, Colorado, and Magdalena) have spotty distributions with one of their centers in the GYE. This group is one of the more easily differentiated. Many species can easily be identified by simple observation and they tend to fly slower than some of their conspecifics, which is a major asset to the novice lepidopterist!

104. THEANO ALPINE (*Erebia theano*) (Plate 14; 1.2–1.4", 31–38mm) Dorsally dark brown w/submarginal dashes of orange or red across both wings. No eyespots. Ventrally FW same as DFW; HW has six to eight ivory dashes which are not circular. Habitat: Bogs below treeline; open pine forest. Nectar: Prefers yellow and white flowers. Host plants: Grasses (Family Poaceae) and sedges (Family Cyperaceae). Eggs laid on willows (*Salix* spp.). Rare in the GYE.

105. COLORADO ALPINE (*Erebia callias*) (Plate 14; 1.3–1.49", 34–38mm) Dorsally brown with reddish FW flush; two prominent and nearly connected eyespots below apex. VHW silvery gray w/minute dark markings crossed by one to two thin irregular lines. Habitat: Meadows above treeline. Food: Nectar and mud. Host plants: Grasses (Family Poaceae) and sedges (Family Cyperaceae) including common bogsedge (*Kobresia myosuroides*). Rare in the GYE.

106. MAGDALENA ALPINE (*Erebia magdalena*) (Plate 14; 1.73–1.9", 44–50mm) As its name implies, this species is all black both dorsally and ventrally with absolutely no markings. Habitat: Rockslides at or above timberline. Host plants: Grasses (Family Poaceae) and sedges (Family Cyperaceae). Specific host plant species unknown.

107. COMMON ALPINE (*Erebia epipsodea*) (Plate 14; 1.75–2", 44.4–50.8mm) Relatively common, and fun to pronounce! This is the only *Erebia* with eyespots on both FWs and HWs. Dorsally dark brown, orange bands containing dark eyespots with white pupils. Two eyespots on FW are larger than others. Ventrally similar to D, but lighter. Habitat: Mountain meadows, bogs, clearings, sage flats, often with aspens. Food: Nectar and mud. Host plant: Unknown, but adults fly near grasses (*Poa* spp.).

108. HAYDEN'S RINGLET (*Coenonympha haydenii*) (Plate 14; 1.3–1.49", 34–38mm) Pronounced "see-no-nym-pha." Here is a signature species for the region, one you'll want to add to your list of observed species. It is habitat specific, living only in the greater Yellowstone area. Dorsally both male and female are a light mustard gray-brown color, and the female is much lighter than the male. VHW has a marginal row of five to seven small eyespots with white centers ringed with buff or yellow. Habitat: Mountain meadows, open forests and trailsides to 9,000 ft. Host plants: Unknown grasses (Family Poaceae).

109. INORNATE COMMON RINGLET (*Coenonympha tullia inornata*) (Plate 14; 1.25–1.375", 31.75–34.9mm) Dorsally dark, brownish tan. VFW mustard yellow with apex and HW heavily scaled with gray or greenish. Eyespots few or absent, but very small eyespot at FW apex present in some individuals. Habitat: Lowland. Host plants: Grasses including Kentucky bluegrass (*Poa pratensis*) and needle-and-thread grass (*Stipa comata*).

110. RIDINGS' SATYR (*Neominois ridingsii*) (Plate 14; 1.4–2", 35–50mm) Gray with pale patches and two black eyespots on forewing. Habitat: Found in very dry sagebrush and prairie sites. Host plants: Blue gramma (*Bouteloua gracilis*) and possibly other grasses.

111. COMMON WOOD-NYMPH (*Cercyonis pegala*) (Plate 15; 1.73–2.7", 44–69mm) Largest of this genus, this species was previously known as the "goggle-eye." Dorsally two large eyespots surrounded by a yellow area; gray-brown elsewhere. Ventrally FW spots largest of all wing surfaces. Zero to six HW eyespots. VHW is a solid brown with no striations, unlike the Great Basin Wood-Nymph (*C. sthelene*). Habitat: Moist areas. Hostplants: Grasses (Family Poaceae) including beardgrass (*Andropogon* spp.), purpletop (*Tridens flavus*), certain *Stipa* species, alkali-grasses (*Puccunellia* spp.), and Kentucky bluegrass (*Poa pratensis*, in the lab).

112. SMALL WOOD-NYMPH (*Cercyonis oetus*) (Plate 15; 1.25–1.75", 31.7–44.45mm) Smaller wood-nymph compared to the Common Wood-Nymph (*C. pegala*). DFW usually one eyespot in male, two in female, with the lower eyespot smaller. Ventrally in both sexes, lower eyespot on FW smaller, nearer to wing margin than upper eyespot. Ground color medium-brown. Postbasal and median lines dark and irregular. Wing fringes are checkered. Habitat: Dry, often elevated grasslands, sagebrush, scrub, meadows, open woodland. Host plants: Unknown grasses (Family Poaceae).

113. GREAT BASIN WOOD-NYMPH (*Cercyonis sthenele*) (Plate 15; 1.3–1.73", 34–44mm) Similar to the Common Wood-Nymph (*C. pegala*), but smaller and VHW has more of a striated pattern resembling tree bark. Basal half of VHW darker; outer edge of dark area irregular. DFW eyespots: male's upper eyespot is larger while female's eyespots are equal in size. Eyespots are equidistant from outer margin. Color varies from light to dark brown. Habitat: Open pine forests and sagebrush. Host plants: Unknown grasses (Family Poaceae).

114. UHLER'S ARCTIC (*Oeneis uhleri*) (Plate 15; 1.5–1.875", 38.1–47.6mm) Dorsally variable shades of mustard brown, FW one to two eyespots, HW ring of one to five eyespots. Ventrally similar to D, HW striated with arcs concentric with margin. Smaller than the Brown Chryxus Arctic (*O. chryxus chryxus*) and lacks FW bird beak design on VFW. Habitat: Pine forest openings in mountains, dry grassy glades, shrubby foothills, sage flats. Host plants: Unknown but probably grasses.

115. BROWN CHRYXUS ARCTIC (*Oeneis chryxus chryxus*) (Plate 15; 1.75–2", 44.45–50.8mm) Dorsally tan to brown close to body, orangish brown outer half of wing, FW has two black spots, HW one black spot. VFW tawny. You may be able to imagine a bird's head with beak pointing away from basal area if you look closely. VHW bark-colored and crossed by broad median band. Habitat: Evergreen forest clearings, mountain meadows, and sage flats. Host plants: Grasses such

as reed canarygrass (*Phalaris arundinacea*) as well as sedges (Family Cyperaceae).

116. WHITE-VEINED ARCTIC (*Oeneis taygete*) (Plate 15; 1.4–1.9", 35–47mm) Wings translucent. Dorsally gray-brown, without eyespots. Ventrally faint brown partial postmedian bar extending down from costa; VHW with strong median dark band outlined in white. Habitat: Tundra, alpine, and bogs. Host plants: Grasses (Family Poaceae) and sedges (Family Cyperaceae).

117. JUTTA ARCTIC (*Oeneis jutta*) (Plate 15; 1.8–2.2", 47–56mm) Distinguished from the Brown Chryxus Arctic (*O. chryxus chryxus*) by evenly mottled VHW (no median line evident) and posterior VFW spot larger than anterior VFW spot. Dorsally HW mottled w/brown. Habitat: Acid bogs and lodgepole forests. Found on trunks of standing living trees. Host plants: Sedges (Family Cyperaceae), and rushes (Family Juncaceae).

118. MELISSA ARCTIC (*Oeneis melissa*) (Plate 15; 1.6–1.7", 41–44mm) Wings slightly translucent. Plain gray-brown, with no eyespots. VHW darker than DHW. Dorsally some veins evident with light submarginal band. Habitat: Elevated tundra and alpine. Host plants: Grasses (Family Poaceae) and sedges (Family Cyperaceae).

## Milkweed Butterflies (Subfamily Danainae)

Another subfamily of the Nymphalidae. Worldwide range, large, usually brightly colored, long-lived. Larvae feed on plants like milkweed, ingesting poisonous juices that are said to make the butterfly unpalatable to other predators. Only one of the Danaidae is a regular visitor to the Yellowstone, but its idea of a sojourn puts our machine-assisted travels to shame!

119. MONARCH (*Danaus plexippus*) (Plate 14; 3.5–4", 88.9–101.6mm) Famous for its long migration from Canada and the United States to Mexico. Orange with black veins and black margins that contain white dots. Habitat: On migration,

anywhere; prefers meadows. Host plants: Milkweeds (Family Asclepiadaceae) and dogbanes (Family Apocynaceae).

## NOTE

1. On the simplification of butterfly taxonomy, see James A. Scott, *The Butterflies of North America* (Stanford University Press, 1986), pp. 116–117.

# Glossary[1]

**Anal veins**: The veins of the hindwing near the anus.
**Anterior**: Behind.
**Apex**: Outer tip of a wing.
**Apical**: Pertains to the apex.

**Basal**: Pertains to the base; most often refers to where the wing attaches to the thorax.
**Border**: A relatively narrow band of color either separating other color patterns, or on the edge of another color pattern.

**Cell**: The area between the wing veins. Usually, descriptions refer to the discal cell, or the area in the middle.
**Chevrons**: Striped or dashed color markings grouped together, often resembling a corporal's or sergeant's stripes.
**Costal**: The leading edge of the wing.

**Dingy**: Faded, dull, or muted coloration.
**Disc, discal area**: The middle or central area of the wing.
**Discal cell**: The central or middle area between wing veins.
**Distal**: Opposite the point of attachment or origin.
**Dorsal**: Pertaining to the back, or upper side of a butterfly.

**Eyespots**: Circular coloration on wing.

**Fell field**: Scottish term traditionally meaning a stretch of elevated wasteland or pasture, a down. For us, that means a productive mountain meadow!

**Marginal**: Pertains to the area located at (or near) the outer edge of the wing.
**Median**: The area halfway between the base and apex or outer edge of the wing.

**Outer margin**: The edge of the wing, located between the apex and the tornus or anal angle. You might think of it as the trailing edge of the wing.
**Overscaling**: Scales of a distinctive color that lie over other scales that display a wing's underlying and basic color.

**Palpus, Palpi**: Insect mouthparts, or facial protrusions on either side of proboscis that protect it.
**Postbasal**: The area just beyond the base of the wings.
**Posterior**: Behind or to the rear.
**Postmedian**: Just beyond the median (toward the apex) or middle of the wing.
**Proximal**: Toward the point of attachment or origin.

**Scales**: Actually fine hairs covering a butterfly's wings. Very delicate and easily damaged by handling.
**Scaling**: Refers to scales, generally used in reference to appearance or patterns.
**Sex scaling**: Scaling determined by sex of butterfly.
**Striated**: Many fine-scale markings on the wing.
**Submarginal**: The location just inward from the outer edge or margin of the wing.
**Submedian**: Between the postbasal and median areas on the wing.
**Subtornal**: Below the tornus.

**Tawny**: Brownish yellow.

**Thorax**: The second part of an insect's body; point of attachment for wings and legs.

**Tornus**: Place where the wing angles, junction of the inner and outer wing margins.

**Vein**: A tubular structure that supports a butterfly's wing.

**Ventral**: Pertaining to the venter or belly, abdominal. In short, the lower or underside of a butterfly.

**Wing bases**: The location near the wing's point of attachment.

## NOTE

1. We acknowledge borrowing from the glossary found in the Peterson Series' *Field Guide to Western Butterflies*, by James W. Tilden and Arthur Clayton Smith (Boston: Houghton Mifflin, 1986), as well as the Peterson Series' *Field Guide to Western Butterflies*, by Paul Opler (Boston: Houghton Mifflin, 1999) and refer readers to this and other excellent guidebooks for more butterfly terms and information.

# Appendix 1

# Essential Reading and Conservation Resources

## OTHER GOOD GUIDEBOOKS TO BUTTERFLIES

An informal and lovely pocket guide is found in *Painted Ladies: Butterflies of North America,* by Millie Miller and Cyndi Nelson (Boulder: Johnson Books, 1993). Excellent references include *Butterflies through Binoculars–The West* by Jeffrey Glassberg (New York: Oxford University Press, 2001) and the *Audubon Society Field Guide to North American Butterflies* (Robert M. Pyle, consulting lepidopterist, Alfred A. Knopf, 1981). The original Peterson Field Guide Series *A Field Guide to Western Butterflies* was written in 1986 by James W. Tilden and Arthur Clayton Smith. The latest edition is authored by Paul A. Opler and Amy Bartlett Wright, also published by Houghton Mifflin (1999). C. D. Bird, G. J. Hilchie, N. G. Kondla, E. M. Pike, and F. A. H. Sperling's *Alberta Butterflies* (Edmonton: The Provincial Museum of Alberta, 1995) is also a relevant resource, as many of the GYE species are present in Alberta and vice versa. A clear guide to recent nomenclature is contained in the North American Butterfly Association's "Checklist & English Names of North American Butterflies Occurring North of Mexico"

(Morristown, NJ: NABA, 2001, available on the web at: *http://www.naba.org/pubs/enames2.html*).

## MORE ABOUT BUTTERFLIES

The very first book you really must read is Robert Michael Pyle's *Handbook for Butterfly Watchers* (Boston: Houghton Mifflin, 1984, 1992). Scientific reference works include *The Lives of Butterflies*, by Matthew M. Douglas (Ann Arbor: University of Michigan Press, 1986), *The Butterflies of North America: A Natural History and Field Guide*, by James A. Scott (Stanford University Press, 1986), and *Butterflies of the Rocky Mountain States*, edited by Clifford D. Ferris and F. Martin Brown (University of Oklahoma Press, 1981). The Lepidopterists' Society has recently published William D. Winter, Jr.'s *Basic Techniques for Observing and Studying Moths and Butterflies*. A solid and encouraging resource to help out in your own backyard is *Butterfly Gardening: Creating Summer Magic in Your Garden* created by The Xerces Society and The Smithsonian Institution (San Francisco: Sierra Club Books, 1998). For the literary, see "Nabokov's Butterflies" by Vladimir Nabokov, *The Atlantic Monthly* 285 (April 2000): 51–75. Clarence M. Weed's *Butterflies Worth Knowing* (New York: Doubleday Page & Co., 1917) is a lovely work in both description and artwork. Other classic books include W. J. Holland's *The Butterfly Book* (New York: Doubleday, Page & Co., 1905), John Adams Comstock and Anna Botsford Comstock's *How to Know the Butterflies* (New York: D. Appleton and Company, 1904), and William Henry Edwards's *The Butterflies of North America*, published in three volumes between 1868 and 1897. Gene Stratton Porter not only wrote about a girl of the Limberlost, but *Moths of the Limberlost* as well (Garden City, New York: Doubleday, Page & Co., 1912). There are many more books, classic and recent, so be sure to check the bibliographies in Pyle's work and other books to find more information and rare treasures in the library.

## HISTORY OF YELLOWSTONE
## NATIONAL PARK AND THE REGION

Many books about Yellowstone Park have been written, so here are just a few good ones to begin with. A lyrical and compelling story of Yellowstone Park is found in *Searching for Yellowstone: Ecology and Wonder in the Last Wilderness,* by Paul Schullery (Boston: Houghton Mifflin, 1997), and a wonderful account of tourism in the park is Judith L. Meyer's *The Spirit of Yellowstone: The Cultural Evolution of a National Park* (Lanham MD: Rowman & Littlefield, 1996). The classic history of the park, *The Yellowstone Story,* by Aubrey L. Haines, remains worthy of time, tea, and a comfortable chair (Yellowstone Library and Museum Association with the Colorado Associated University Press, 1977). For the history of Grand Teton National Park, see *Crucible for Conservation,* by Robert Righter (Colorado Associated University Press, 1982). On the Hayden expedition of 1871, see Marlene D. Merrill's *Yellowstone and the Great West* (Lincoln: University of Nebraska Press, 1999).

### SCIENCE AND RESOURCE MANAGEMENT

Titles relating to the history of resource or wildlife management in Yellowstone include R. Gerald Wright's *Wildlife Research and Management in the National Parks* (Urbana: University of Illinois Press, 1992), Richard West Sellars's *Preserving Nature in the National Parks: A History* (New Haven: Yale University Press, 1997), and James A. Pritchard's *Preserving Yellowstone's Natural Conditions: Science and the Perception of Nature* (Lincoln: University of Nebraska Press, 1999). A useful starting point regarding discussions over resource management is *The Greater Yellowstone Ecosystem: Redefining America's Wilderness Heritage,* edited by Robert B. Keiter and Mark S. Boyce (New Haven: Yale University Press, 1991). We recommend a bi-weekly newspaper that covers resource conservation issues in the American West, *High Country News* (Paonia, Colorado, phone 800-905-1155).

## NATURALISTS

Robert Michael Pyle's article, "The Rise and Fall of Natural History" (*Orion* Autumn 2001: 17–23) echoes recent calls for a re-awakening of the naturalist's broad perspective and field experience. Some of our favorite books that capture the spirit of the early naturalists include Howard Ensign Evans's *Pioneer Naturalists: The Discovery and Naming of North American Plants and Animals* (New York: Henry Holt, 1993), Clare Lloyd's *The Traveling Naturalists* (London: Croom Helm, 1985), Alan C. Jenkins's *The Naturalists: Pioneers of Natural History* (New York: Mayflower Books, 1978), and *Magnificent Voyagers: The U.S. Exploring Expedition, 1838–1842*, edited by Herman J. Viola and Carolyn Margolis (Washington, DC: Smithsonian Institution Press, 1985).

## BOOKSELLERS

While you are in the Yellowstone region, be sure to patronize the fine local establishments, including Magpie Books in Three Forks, Vargo's Books and The Country Bookshelf in Bozeman, and The Book Peddler in West Yellowstone, Montana. On the Wyoming side of the ecosystem, check out The Buffalo Bill Historical Center in Cody, Main Street Books in Lander, and Valley Bookstore in Jackson. In the parks, visit the splendid bookshops operated by the Yellowstone Association and the Grand Teton Natural History Association. Unfortunately, Patricia Ledlie Bookseller, of Buckfield, Maine, has closed shop, and it appears that the Stonecrop Natural History Book Catalog of Denver, Colorado, also has ceased doing business. But there is yet hope for bibliophiles; support your local independent bookseller, and the specialty bookshops! Try searching with your Internet browser using key words like "natural history books." Here are two promising shops we found: Gary Wayner Bookseller, *www.wayner.com* and The Outdoor Bookstore, of Libby, Montana, *www.outdoorbooks.com.*

## CONSERVATION ORGANIZATIONS
## AND WEBSITE REFERENCES

We list a few conservation and educational organizations pertinent to butterflies and to the region. Find out more about them by looking up their website, or by requesting information and a recent newsletter.

The Xerces Society
4828 Southeast Hawthorne Blvd.
Portland, OR 97215
*xerces@teleport.com*
fax 503.233.6794
*www.xerces.org*
Publishes *Wings* twice a year

North American Butterfly Association
4 Delaware Rd.
Morristown, NJ 07960
800-503-2290
*www.naba.org*
Publishes the quarterlies *American Butterflies* and *Butterfly Garden News*

Lepidopterists' Society
1608 Presidio Way
Roseville, CA 95661
*www.furman.edu/~snyder/snyder/lep*

Yellowstone Geographic website
This website features natural history-oriented information about the region; well worth a visit.
*www.yellowstonegeographic.com*

Greater Yellowstone Coalition
13 S. Wilson
Bozeman, MT 50715
406-586-1593
*www.greateryellowstone.org*

Montana Wilderness Society
P.O. Box 635
Helena, MT 59624
*mwa@desktop.org*

Northern Rockies Conservation Cooperative
P.O. Box 2705
Jackson, WY 83001
307-733-6856

Grand Teton Natural History Association
Grand Teton National Park
Moose, Wyoming 83012
*www.grandtetonpark.org*

Yellowstone Association
P.O. Box 117
Yellowstone National Park, WY 82190
307-344-2296
*www.YellowstoneAssociation.org*

The Yellowstone Institute
P.O. Box 117
Yellowstone National Park, Wyoming 82190
*http://www.yellowstone.net/instit.htm*

Teton Science School
(in Grand Teton National Park)
P.O. Box 68,
Kelly, WY 83011
307-733-4765 Fax 307-739-9388
*http://www.tetonscience.org/*
Email: info@tetonscience.org

The Nature Conservancy
1815 Lynn St.
Arlington, VA 22209
*www.tnc.org*

## EQUIPMENT SUPPLIERS

BioQuip Products (equipment catalogue for sources of nets, forceps, collecting envelopes, etc.)
17803 LaSalle Ave.
Gardena, CA 90248-3602, USA
301-324-0620
Email: bioquip@aol.com

# Appendix 2

# Checklist for Butterflies of Grand Teton National Park, Teton County, Wyoming

**SWALLOWTAILS (FAMILY PAPILIONIDAE)**
**Parnassians (Subfamily Parnassiinae)**
\_\_\_\_ Clodius Parnassian (*Parnassius clodius*)
\_\_\_\_ Rocky Mountain Phoebus Parnassian (*Parnassius phoebus smintheus*)

**Swallowtails (Subfamily Papilioninae)**
\_\_\_\_ Pale Swallowtail (*Papilio eurymedon*)
\_\_\_\_ Old World Swallowtail (*Papilio machaon*)
\_\_\_\_ Anise Swallowtail (*Papilio zelicaon*)
\_\_\_\_ Western Tiger Swallowtail (*Papilio rutulus*)
\_\_\_\_ Two-Tailed Tiger Swallowtail (*Papilio multicaudata*)

**WHITES AND SULPHURS (FAMILY PIERIDAE)**
**Whites (Subfamily Pierinae)**
\_\_\_\_ Becker's White (*Pontia beckerii*) [just outside of park boundary]
\_\_\_\_ Spring White (*Pontia sisymbrii*)
\_\_\_\_ Checkered White (*Pontia protodice*)
\_\_\_\_ Western White (*Pontia occidentalis*)
\_\_\_\_ Margined Mustard White (*Pieris napi marginalis*)

____ Cabbage White (*Pieris rapae*)
____ Large Marble (*Euchloe ausonides*)
____ Desert Pearly Marble (*Euchloe hyantis lotta*)
____ Stella Sara Orangetip (*Anthocharis sara stella*)

## Sulphurs (Subfamily Coliadinae)
____ Clouded Sulphur (*Colias philodice*)
____ Orange Sulphur (*Colias eurytheme*)
____ Queen Alexandra's Sulphur (*Colias alexandra*)
____ Christina's Sulphur (*Colias christina*)
____ Mead's Sulphur (*Colias meadii*)
____ Giant Sulphur (*Colias gigantea*)
____ Pink-edged Sulphur (*Colias interior*)
____ Pelidne Sulphur (*Colias pelidne*)

## GOSSAMER-WING BUTTERFLIES (FAMILY LYCAENIDAE)
## Coppers (Subfamily Lycaeninae)
____ Bronze Copper (*Lycaena hyllus*)
____ Edith's Copper (*Lycaena editha*)
____ Ruddy Copper (*Lycaena rubidus*)
____ Blue Copper (*Lycaena heteronea*)
____ Purplish Copper (*Lycaena helloides*)
____ Lilac-bordered Copper (*Lycaena nivalis*)
____ Lustrous Copper (*Lycaena cupreus*)
____ Mariposa Copper (*Lycaena mariposa*)

## Hairstreaks (Subfamily Theclinae)
____ Coral Hairstreak (*Satyrium titus*)
____ Sooty Hairstreak (*Satyrium fuliginosa*)
____ Acadian Hairstreak (*Satyrium acadica*)
____ Sylvan Hairstreak (*Satyrium sylvinus*)
____ Hedgerow Hairstreak (*Satyrium saepium*)
____ Bramble Hairstreak (*Callophrys dumetorum*)
____ Sheridan's Hairstreak (*Callophrys sheridanii*)
____ Western Pine Elfin (*Callophrys eryphon*)

## Blues (Subfamily Polyommatinae)
____ Western Tailed-Blue (*Everes amyntula*)
____ Dotted Blue (*Euphilotes enoptes ancilla*)
____ Arrowhead Blue (*Glaucopsyche piasus*)
____ Silvery Blue (*Glaucopsyche lygdamus*)
____ Northern Blue (*Lycaeides idas*)
____ Melissa Blue (*Lycaeides melissa*)
____ Greenish Blue (*Plebejus saepiolus*)
____ Boisduval's Blue (*Plebejus icarioides*)
____ Shasta Blue (*Plebejus shasta*)
____ Lupine Blue (*Plebejus lupini*)
____ Arctic Blue (*Agriades glandon*)

## BRUSHFOOTED BUTTERFLIES (FAMILY NYMPHALIDAE)
## Heliconians and Fritillaries (Subfamily Heliconiinae)
____ Great Spangled Fritillary (*Speyeria cybele*)
____ Coronis Fritillary (*Speyeria coronis*)
____ Zerene Fritillary (*Speyeria zerene*)
____ Callippe Fritillary (*Speyeria callippe*)
____ Great Basin Fritillary (*Speyeria egleis*)
____ Hesperis Atlantis Fritillary (*Speyeria atlantis hesperis*)
____ Hydaspe Fritillary (*Speyeria hydaspe*)
____ Mormon Fritillary (*Speyeria mormonia*)
____ Silver-bordered Fritillary (*Boloria selene*)
____ Frigga Fritillary (*Boloria frigga*)
____ Relict Fritillary (*Boloria kriemhild*)
____ Freija Fritillary (*Boloria freija*)
____ Arctic Fritillary (*Boloria chariclea*)

## True Brushfoots (Subfamily Nymphalinae)
____ Northern Checkerspot (*Chlosyne palla*)
____ Sagebrush Checkerspot (*Chlosyne acastus*)
____ Northern Crescent (*Phyciodes selenis*)
____ Field Crescent (*Phyciodes campestris*)
____ Mylitta Crescent (*Phyciodes mylitta*)

____ Gillett's Checkerspot (*Euphydryas gillettii*)
____ Variable Checkerspot (*Euphydryas chalcedona*)
____ Edith's Checkerspot (*Euphydryas editha*)
____ Satyr Comma (*Polygonia satyrus*)
____ Green Comma (*Polygonia faunus*)
____ Hoary Comma (*Polygonia gracilis*)
____ Oreas Comma (*Polygonia oreas*)
____ California Tortoiseshell (*Nymphalis californica*)
____ Mourning Cloak (*Nymphalis antiopa*)
____ Milbert's Tortoiseshell (*Nymphalis milberti*)
____ Painted Lady (*Vanessa cardui*)
____ West Coast Lady (*Vanessa annabella*)
____ Red Admiral (*Vanessa atalanta*)

## Admirals and Relatives (Subfamily Limenitidinae)
____ Weidemeyer's Admiral (*Limenitis weidemeyerii*)

## Satyrs (Subfamily Satyrinae)
____ Hayden's Ringlet (*Coenonympha haydenii*)
____ Inornate Common Ringlet (*Coenonympha tullia inornata*)
____ Common Wood-Nymph (*Cercyonis pegala*)
____ Great Basin Wood-Nymph (*Cercyonis sthenele*)
____ Small Wood-Nymph (*Cercyonis oetus*)
____ Common Alpine (*Erebia epipsodea*)
____ Brown Chryxus Arctic (*Oeneis chryxus chryxus*)
____ Uhler's Arctic (*Oeneis uhleri*)

## Monarchs (Subfamily Danainae)
____ Monarch (*Danaus plexippus*)

## NOTE

This species list is adapted from Diane M. Debinski and Paul A. Opler's Checklist for Butterflies of Grand Teton National Park, Teton County, Wyoming, October 10, 2001, *http://www.npwrc.usgs.gov/ resource/1999/insect/gteton.htm*

# Appendix 3

# Checklist for Butterflies of Yellowstone National Park, Wyoming

**SWALLOWTAILS (FAMILY PAPILIONIDAE)**
**Parnassians (Subfamily Parnassiinae)**
\_\_\_\_ Clodius Parnassian (*Parnassius clodius*)
\_\_\_\_ Rocky Mountain Phoebus Parnassian (*Parnassius phoebus smintheus*)

**Swallowtails (Subfamily Papilioninae)**
\_\_\_\_ Old World Swallowtail (*Papilio machaon*)
\_\_\_\_ Western Tiger Swallowtail (*Papilio rutulus*)
\_\_\_\_ Two-tailed Swallowtail (*Papilio multicaudata*)
\_\_\_\_ Pale Swallowtail (*Papilio eurymedon*)

**WHITES AND SULPHURS (FAMILY PIERIDAE)**
**Whites (Subfamily Pierinae)**
\_\_\_\_ Becker's White (*Pontia beckerii*)
\_\_\_\_ Spring White (*Pontia sisymbrii*)
\_\_\_\_ Checkered White (*Pontia protodice*)
\_\_\_\_ Western White (*Pontia occidentalis*)
\_\_\_\_ Margined Mustard White (*Pieris napi marginalis*)
\_\_\_\_ Cabbage White (*Pieris rapae*)

____ Large Marble (*Euchloe ausonides*)
____ Stella Sara Orangetip (*Anthocharis sara stella*)

## Sulphurs (Subfamily Coliadinae)
____ Clouded Sulphur (*Colias philodice*)
____ Orange Sulphur (*Colias eurytheme*)
____ Christina's Sulphur (*Colias christina*)
____ Queen Alexandra's Sulphur (*Colias alexandra*)
____ Mead's Sulphur (*Colias meadii*)
____ Giant Sulphur (*Colias gigantea*)
____ Pelidne Sulphur (*Colias pelidne*)

## GOSSAMER-WING BUTTERFLIES (FAMILY LYCAENIDAE)
## Coppers (Subfamily Lycaeninae)
____ American Copper (*Lycaena phlaeas*)
____ Lustrous Copper (*Lycaena cupreus*)
____ Edith's Copper (*Lycaena editha*)
____ Ruddy Copper (*Lycaena rubidus*)
____ Blue Copper (*Lycaena heteronea*)
____ Purplish Copper (*Lycaena helloides*)
____ Lilac-bordered Copper (*Lycaena nivalis*)
____ Mariposa Copper (*Lycaena mariposa*)

## Hairstreaks (Subfamily Theclinae)
____ Coral Hairstreak (*Satyrium titus*)
____ Sooty Hairstreak (*Satyrium fuliginosa*)
____ California Hairstreak (*Satyrium californica*)
____ Sylvan Hairstreak (*Satyrium sylvinus*)
____ Hedgerow Hairstreak (*Satyrium saepium*)
____ Bramble Hairstreak (*Callophrys dumetorum*)
____ Sheridan's Hairstreak (*Callophrys sheridanii*)
____ Western Pine Elfin (*Callophrys eryphon*)
____ Thicket Hairstreak (*Callophrys spinetorum*)

## Blues (Subfamily Polyommatinae)
____ Western Tailed-Blue (*Everes amyntula*)
____ Spring Azure (*Celastrina ladon*)

____ Arrowhead Blue (*Glaucopsyche piasus*)
____ Silvery Blue (*Glaucopsyche lygdamus*)
____ Northern Blue (*Lycaeides idas*)
____ Melissa Blue (*Lycaeides melissa*)
____ Greenish Blue (*Plebejus saepiolus*)
____ Boisduval's Blue (*Plebejus icarioides*)
____ Shasta Blue (*Plebejus shasta*)
____ Lupine Blue (*Plebejus lupini*)
____ Arctic Blue (*Agriades glandon*)

## BRUSHFOOTED BUTTERFLIES (FAMILY NYMPHALIDAE)
### Heliconians and Fritillaries (Subfamily Heliconiinae)
____ Great Spangled Fritillary (*Speyeria cybele*)
____ Aphrodite Fritillary (*Speyeria aphrodite*)
____ Edwards' Fritillary (*Speyeria edwardsii*)
____ Coronis Fritillary (*Speyeria coronis*)
____ Zerene Fritillary (*Speyeria zerene*)
____ Callippe Fritillary (*Speyeria callippe*)
____ Great Basin Fritillary (*Speyeria egleis*)
____ Hydaspe Fritillary (*Speyeria hydaspe*)
____ Mormon Fritillary (*Speyeria mormonia*)
____ Silver-bordered Fritillary (*Boloria selene*)
____ Frigga Fritillary (*Boloria frigga*)
____ Relict Fritillary (*Boloria kriemhild*)
____ Meadow Fritillary (*Boloria bellona*)
____ Freija Fritillary (*Boloria freija*)
____ Arctic Fritillary (*Boloria chariclea*)

### True Brushfoots (Subfamily Nymphalinae)
____ Northern Checkerspot (*Chlosyne palla*)
____ Northern Crescent (*Phyciodes selenis*)
____ Field Crescent (*Phyciodes campestris*)
____ Pale Crescent (*Phyciodes pallida*)
____ Gillett's Checkerspot (*Euphydryas gillettii*)
____ Variable Checkerspot (*Euphydryas chalcedona*)
____ Edith's Checkerspot (*Euphydryas editha*)
____ Satyr Comma (*Polygonia satyrus*)

\_\_\_\_ Green Comma (*Polygonia faunus*)
\_\_\_\_ Hoary Comma (*Polygonia gracilis*)
\_\_\_\_ California Tortoiseshell (*Nymphalis californica*)
\_\_\_\_ Mourning Cloak (*Nymphalis antiopa*)
\_\_\_\_ Milbert's Tortoiseshell (*Nymphalis milberti*)
\_\_\_\_ Painted Lady (*Vanessa cardui*)
\_\_\_\_ West Coast Lady (*Vanessa annabella*)
\_\_\_\_ Red Admiral (*Vanessa atalanta*)

## Admirals and Relatives (Subfamily Limenitidinae)
\_\_\_\_ Weidemeyer's Admiral (*Limenitis weidemeyerii*)

## Satyrs (Subfamily Satyrinae)
\_\_\_\_ Hayden's Ringlet (*Coenonympha haydenii*)
\_\_\_\_ Inornate Common Ringlet (*Coenonympha tullia inornata*)
\_\_\_\_ Common Wood-Nymph (*Cercyonis pegala*)
\_\_\_\_ Small Wood-Nymph (*Cercyonis oetus*)
\_\_\_\_ Magdalena Alpine (*Erebia magdalena*)
\_\_\_\_ Theano Alpine (*Erebia theano*)
\_\_\_\_ Colorado Alpine (*Erebia callias*)
\_\_\_\_ Common Alpine (*Erebia epipsodea*)
\_\_\_\_ Ridings' Satyr (*Neominois ridingsii*)
\_\_\_\_ Brown Chryxus Arctic (*Oeneis chryxus chryxus*)
\_\_\_\_ Uhler's Arctic (*Oeneis uhleri*)
\_\_\_\_ Jutta Arctic (*Oeneis jutta*)
\_\_\_\_ Melissa Arctic (*Oeneis melissa*)

## Monarchs (Subfamily Danainae)
\_\_\_\_ Monarch (*Danaus plexippus*)

## NOTE

This species list is adapted from Northern Prairie Wildlife Research Center's Checklist for Butterflies of Yellowstone National Park, Wyoming, *http://www.npwrc.usgs.gov/resource/distr/lepid/bflyusa/chklist/states/counties/wy_88.htm*

# Appendix 4

# List of Butterflies in Numerical/Taxonomic Order with Plate Number

1. Parnassius clodius (F & M)      Plate #2
2. Parnassius phoebus smintheus (F & M)      Plate #2

3. Papilio eurymedon      Plate #1
4. Papilio machaon      Plate #1
5. Papilio canadensis      Plate #1
6. Papilio multicaudata      Plate #1
7. Papilio rutulus      Plate #1
8. Papilio zelicaon      Plate #1

9. Pontia occidentalis (F & M)      Plate #2
10. Pontia protodice (F & M)      Plate #2
11. Pontia sisymbrii      Plate #2
12. Pontia beckerii      Plate #2
13. Neophasia menapia      Plate #2

14. Pieris napi marginalis (F & M)      Plate #3
15. Pieris rapae (F & M)      Plate #3
16. Euchloe olympia      Plate #3
17. Euchloe ausonides      Plate #3
18. Euchloe hyantis lotta      Plate #3
19. Anthocharis sara stella (F & M)      Plate #3

20. Colias pelidne (F & M)                Plate #4
21. Colias meadii (F & M)                 Plate #4
22. Colias gigantea (F & M)               Plate #4
23. Colias philodice (F & M)              Plate #4
24. Colias christina (F & M)              Plate #4

25. Colias alexandra (F & M)              Plate #16

26. Colias interior (F & M)               Plate #4
27. Colias eurytheme (F & M)              Plate #4

28. Euphilotes enoptes ancilla (F & M)    Plate #5
29. Celastrina ladon                      Plate #5
30. Everes amyntula                       Plate #5

31. Plebejus shasta (F & M)               Plate #8
32. Lycaeides idas                        Plate #8
33. Plebejus lupini                       Plate #8
34. Lycaeides melissa                     Plate #8
35. Plebejus saepiolus (F & M)            Plate #8
36. Plebejus icarioides (F & M)           Plate #8
37. Agriades glandon                      Plate #8
38. Glaucopsyche piasus                   Plate #8
39. Glaucopsyche lygdamus                 Plate #8

40. Satyrium behrii                       Plate #5
41. Satyrium saepium                      Plate #5
42. Satyrium californica                  Plate #5
43. Satyrium titus                        Plate #5
44. Satyrium fuliginosa                   Plate #5
45. Satyrium sylvinus                     Plate #5

46. Satyrium acadica                      Plate #16

47. Callophrys sheridanii                 Plate #6
48. Callophrys dumetorum                  Plate #6
49. Callophrys polios                     Plate #6
50. Callophrys augustinus                 Plate #6
51. Callophrys gryneus                    Plate #6
52. Callophrys eryphon (F & M)            Plate #6
53. Callophrys spinetorum                 Plate #6
54. Lycaena rubidus (M)                   Plate #6

| | |
|---|---|
| 54. Lycaena rubidus (F) | Plate #16 |
| 55. Lycaena hyllus (M & F) | Plate #16 |
| 56. Lycaena helloides (F & M) | Plate #7 |
| 57. Lycaena mariposa (F & M) | Plate #7 |
| 58. Lycaena nivalis (F & M) | Plate #7 |
| 59. Lycaena cupreus | Plate #7 |
| 60. Lycaena heteronea (F & M) | Plate #7 |
| 61. Lycaena phlaeas | Plate #7 |
| 62. Lycaena editha (M) | Plate #16 |
| 63. Lycaena dione | Plate #7 |
| 64. Speyeria aphrodite | Plate #12 |
| 65. Speyeria cybele | Plate #12 |
| 66. Speyeria atlantis hesperis | Plate #11 |
| 67. Speyeria hydaspe | Plate #11 |
| 68. Speyeria callippe | Plate #11 |
| 69. Speyeria zerene | Plate #11 |
| 70. Speyeria edwardsii | Plate #11 |
| 71. Speyeria egleis | Plate #11 |
| 72. Speyeria coronis | Plate #11 |
| 73. Speyeria mormonia | Plate #11 |
| 74. Boloria freija | Plate #16 |
| 75. Boloria frigga | Plate #12 |
| 76. Boloria bellona | Plate #12 |
| 77. Boloria kriemhild | Plate #12 |
| 78. Boloria selene | Plate #12 |
| 79. Boloria eunomia | Plate #12 |
| 80. Boloria chariclea | Plate #12 |
| 81. Phyciodes mylitta | Plate #10 |
| 82. Phyciodes campestris | Plate #10 |
| 83. Phyciodes selenis (M & F) | Plate #10 |
| 84. Phyciodes pallida | Plate #10 |
| 85. Chlosyne acastus | Plate #13 |
| 86. Chlosyne palla | Plate #13 |
| 87. Chlosyne gorgone | Plate #13 |

| | | |
|---|---|---|
| 88. | Euphydryas editha | Plate #13 |
| 89. | Euphydryas chalcedona | Plate #13 |
| 90. | Euphydryas gillettii | Plate #13 |
| 91. | Polygonia gracilis | Plate #10 |
| 92. | Polygonia oreas | Plate #10 |
| 93. | Polygonia satyrus | Plate #10 |
| 94. | Polygonia faunus | Plate #10 |
| 95. | Nymphalis milberti | Plate #9 |
| 96. | Nymphalis californica | Plate #9 |
| 97. | Nymphalis vaualbum | Plate #9 |
| 98. | Nymphalis antiopa | Plate #9 |
| 99. | Vanessa cardui | Plate #9 |
| 100. | Vanessa annabella | Plate #9 |
| 101. | Vanessa atalanta | Plate #9 |
| 102. | Limenitis weidemeyerii | Plate #9 |
| 103. | Limenitis archippus | Plate #9 |
| 104. | Erebia theano | Plate #14 |
| 105. | Erebia callias | Plate #14 |
| 106. | Erebia magdalena | Plate #14 |
| 107. | Erebia epipsodea | Plate #14 |
| 108. | Coenonympha haydenii | Plate #14 |
| 109. | Coenonympha tullia inornata | Plate #14 |
| 110. | Neominois ridingsii | Plate #14 |
| 111. | Cercyonis pegala | Plate #15 |
| 112. | Cercyonis oetus (F) | Plate #15 |
| 113. | Cercyonis sthenele (M) | Plate #15 |
| 114. | Oeneis uhleri (F & M) | Plate #15 |
| 115. | Oeneis chryxus chryxus | Plate #15 |
| 116. | Oeneis taygete | Plate #15 |
| 117. | Oeneis jutta | Plate #15 |
| 118. | Oeneis melissa | Plate #15 |
| 119. | Danaus plexippus | Plate #14 |

# Index

# Plate 1

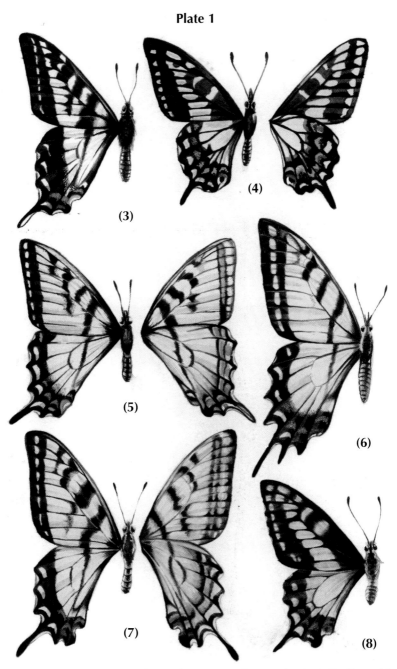

*3. Papilio eurymedon. 4. Papilio machaon. 5. Papilio canadensis. 6. Papilio multi-caudata. 7. Papilio rutulus. 8. Papilio zelicaon.*

# Plate 2

(9)*F*     (9)*M*     (11)

(12)     (10)*F*

(1)*M*     (1)*F*     (10)*M*

(2)*M*     (2)*F*     (13)

9. *Pontia occidentalis.* 11. *Pontia sisymbrii.* 12. *Pontia beckerii.* 10. *Pontia protodice.* 1. *Parnassius clodius.* 2. *Parnassius phoebus smintheus.* 13. *Neophasia menapia.*

# Plate 3

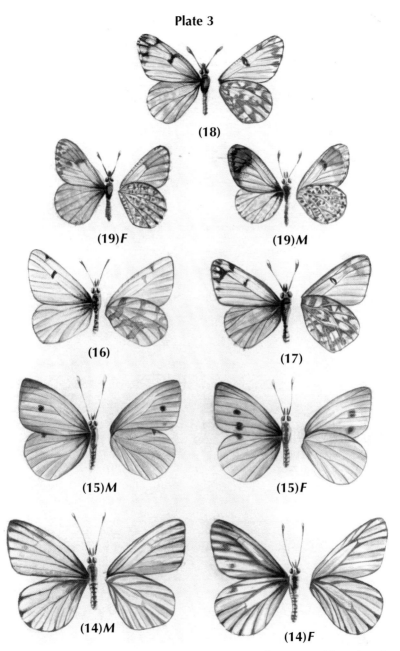

(18)

(19)*F*                    (19)*M*

(16)                    (17)

(15)*M*                    (15)*F*

(14)*M*                    (14)*F*

*18. Euchloe hyantis lotta. 19. Anthocharis sara stella. 16. Euchloe olympia. 17. Euchloe ausonides. 15. Pieris rapae. 14. Pieris napi marginalis.*

# Plate 4

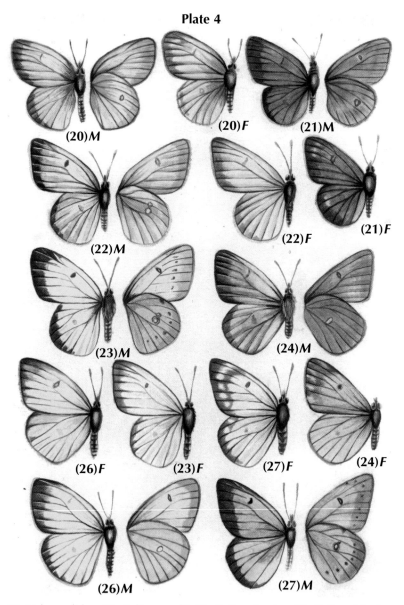

(20)M

(20)F

(21)M

(22)M

(22)F

(21)F

(23)M

(24)M

(26)F

(23)F

(27)F

(24)F

(26)M

(27)M

20. *Colias pelidne.* 21. *Colias meadii.* 22. *Colias gigantea.* 23. *Colias philodice.*
24. *Colias christina.* 26. *Colias interior.* 27. *Colias eurytheme.*

# Plate 5

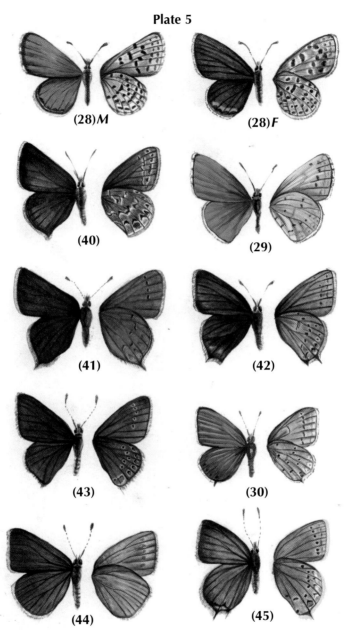

(28)*M*

(28)*F*

(40)

(29)

(41)

(42)

(43)

(30)

(44)

(45)

28. *Euphilotes enoptes ancilla.* 40. *Satyrium behrii.* 29. *Celastrina ladon.*
41. *Satyrium saepium.* 42. *Satyrium californica.* 43. *Satyrium titus.* 30. *Everes amyntula.* 44. *Satyrium fuliginosa.* 45. *Satyrium sylvinus.*

## Plate 6

(47)  (48)  (49)

(50)  (51)

(52)*M*  (52)*F*

(54)*M*  (53)

47. *Callophrys sheridanii.* 48. *Callophrys dumetorum.* 49. *Callophrys polios.* 50. *Callophrys augustinus.* 51. *Callophrys gryneus.* 52. *Callophrys eryphon.* 54. *Lycaena rubidus.* 53. *Callophrys spinetorum.*

# Plate 7

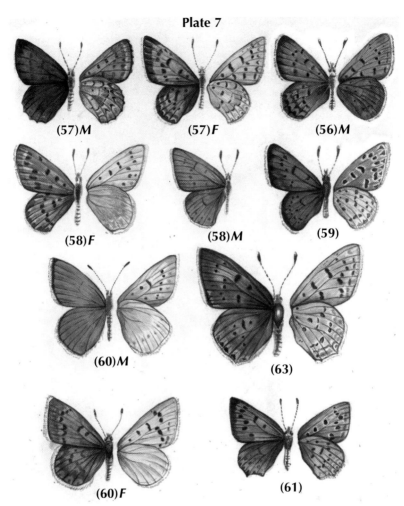

(57)*M*    (57)*F*    (56)*M*

(58)*F*    (58)*M*    (59)

(60)*M*    (63)

(60)*F*    (61)

*57. Lycaena mariposa. 56. Lycaena helloides. 58. Lycaena nivalis. 59. Lycaena cupreus. 60. Lycaena heteronea. 63. Lycaena dione. 61. Lycaena phlaeas.*

# Plate 8

(31)*M*  (31)*F*  (32)  (33)*M*  (34)*M*  (35)*M*  (35)*F*  (37)*M*  (36)*M*  (36)*F*  (38)  (39)

*31. Plebejus shasta. 32. Lycaeides idas. 33. Plebejus lupini. 34. Lycaeides melissa. 35. Plebejus saepiolus. 37. Agriades glandon. 36. Plebejus icarioides. 38. Glaucopsyche piasus. 39. Glaucopsyche lygdamus.*

# Plate 9

(100)

(96)

(101)

(97)

(95)

(103)

(99)

(102)

(98)

100. *Vanessa annabella.* 96. *Nymphalis californica.* 101. *Vanessa atalanta.* 97. *Nymphalis vaualbum.* 95. *Nymphalis milberti.* 99. *Vanessa cardui.* 103. *Limenitis archippus.* 102. *Limenitis weidemeyerii.* 98. *Nymphalis antiopa.*

# Plate 10

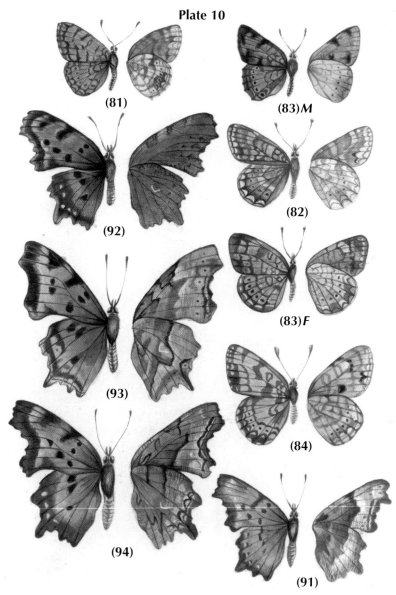

81. *Phyciodes mylitta.* 83. *Phyciodes selenis.* 92. *Polygonia oreas.* 82. *Phyciodes campestris.* 93. *Polygonia satyrus.* 84. *Phyciodes pallida.* 94. *Polygonia faunus.* 91. *Polygonia gracilis.*

# Plate 11

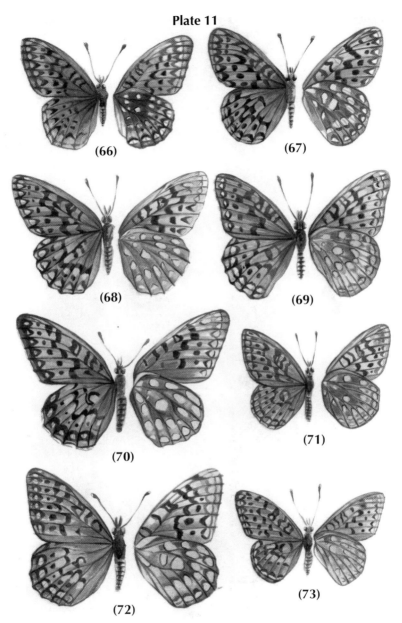

66. *Speyeria atlantis hesperis.* 67. *Speyeria hydaspe.* 68. *Speyeria callippe.* 69. *Speyeria zerene.* 70. *Speyeria edwardsii.* 71. *Speyeria egleis.* 72. *Speyeria coronis.* 73. *Speyeria mormonia.*

# Plate 12

(75)

(76)

(79)

(77)

(80)

(78)

(65)*F*

(64)

*75. Boloria frigga. 76. Boloria bellona. 79. Boloria eunomia. 77. Boloria kriemhild. 80. Boloria chariclea. 78. Boloria selene. 65. Speyeria cybele. 64. Speyeria aphrodite.*

# Plate 13

(86)    (87)

(88)    (85)

(89)    (90)

*86. Chlosyne palla. 87. Chlosyne gorgone. 88. Euphydryas editha. 85. Chlosyne acastus. 89. Euphydryas chalcedona. 90. Euphydryas gillettii.*

# Plate 14

(104)

(105)

(108)

(106)

(107)

(110)

(119)

(109)

104. *Erebia theano.* 105. *Erebia callias.* 108. *Coenonympha haydenii.* 106. *Erebia magdalena.* 107. *Erebia epipsodea.* 110. *Neominois ridingsii.* 119. *Danaus plexippus.* 109. *Coenonympha tullia inornata.*

# Plate 15

113. *Cercyonis sthenele.* 114. *Oeneis uhleri.* 116. *Oeneis taygete.* 112. *Cercyonis oetus.* 117. *Oeneis jutta.* 118. *Oeneis melissa.* 111. *Cercyonis pegala.* 115. *Oeneis chryxus chryxus.*

## Plate 16

(74)

(46)

(25)*M*

(25)*F*

(54)*F*

(62)*M*

(55)*M*

(55)*F*

*74. Boloria freija. 46. Satyrium acadica. 25. Colias alexandra. 54. Lycaena rubidus.*
*62. Lycaena editha. 55. Lycaena hyllus.*